Grit and Grace

How the Pursuit of Mental Toughness and Emotional Intelligence Changes Everything

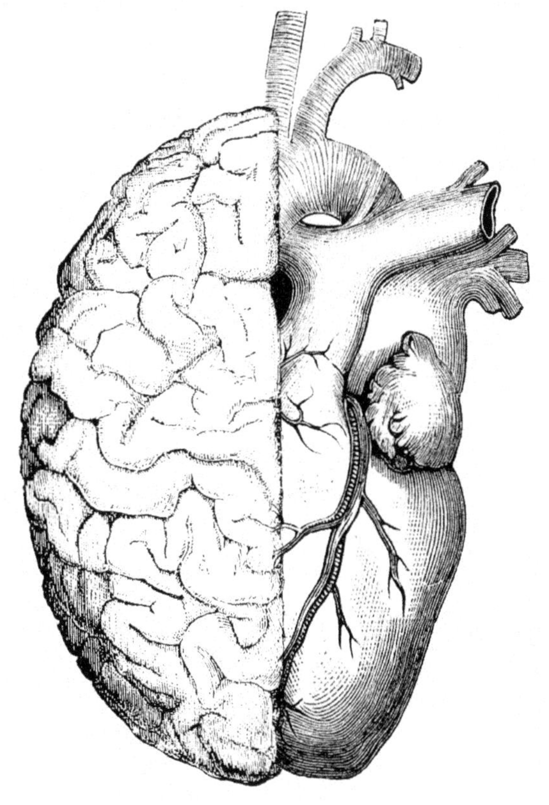

Jeff D. Standridge, Ed.D.

Also by Jeff D. Standridge

Books

Creating Startup Junkies
Building Sustainable Venture Ecosystems in Unexpected Places (with Jeff Amerine)

The Innovator's Field Guide
Accelerators for Entrepreneurs, Innovators, and Change Agents

The Top Performer's Field Guide
Catalysts for Leaders, Superstars, and All Who Aspire to Be

The Abundance Principle
Five Keys to Extraordinary Living
(with Tim Kellerman)

Grit and Grace

How the Pursuit of Mental Toughness and Emotional Intelligence Changes Everything

Jeff D. Standridge, Ed.D.

Published by:

High Point Publishers
1320 Oak St.
Conway, AR 72034

Library of Congress Cataloging-in-Publication Data

Standridge, Jeff D.

ISBN: 978-0-9779-3407-2

LCCN: 2025906814

Printed in the United States of America

1 2 3 4 5 6 7 8 9 10

Legal & Disclaimer

Acknowledgments

To the executives, leaders, colleagues, teammates, friends, and family members who have poured into me and my personal development over the past four decades I say, **"Thank you!"** I simply would not be where I am today and I would not have the opportunity to do the things I do without your feedback, your mentoring, your coaching, your leadership, and most of all, your patience.

Table of Contents

About Jeff D. Standridge, Ed.D.

Dr. Jeff D. Standridge helps organizations, and their leaders generate sustained results in the areas of innovation, strategy, profit growth, organizational transformation, and leadership.

Formally trained as a Paramedic and a Respiratory Therapist, Jeff spent nine years on the Angel One Helicopter Team at Arkansas Children's Hospital, six of which he also served as an Assistant Professor at the University of Arkansas for Medical Sciences. He holds the Doctor of Education degree with special work in Leadership and Organizational Behavior, and a Master of Education degree with special work in Adult Education and Human Resource Development, both from the University of Arkansas – Little Rock. In 2002, Jeff retired from the U.S. Army, Arkansas Army National Guard.

Jeff served for almost two decades with Acxiom Corporation (www.Acxiom.com) where he learned the fine art of leadership, organizational effectiveness, and mergers & acquisitions. In his role as a Group Vice President, Jeff led existing and startup companies in North and South America, Europe, Asia, and the Middle East before leaving in 2016 to focus on coaching, consulting, and investing.

Jeff currently serves as founder and managing director for the Conductor (www.ARConductor.org), as well as for Innovation Junkie (www.InnovationJunkie.com). He is a co-founder and managing partner of Cadron Capital Partners (www.CadronCapital.com) and teaches in the College of Business at the University of Central Arkansas (www.UCA.edu). He comes to the world of consulting, coaching, and innovation, leveraging his experience as an Intrapreneur, Operator, Change Agent, and Investor.

Jeff has been an invited speaker, trainer, and consultant for numerous companies, institutions, and organizations across five continents. He is the author or co-author of four books, three of which have become best sellers. His four books include *The Abundance Principal: Five Keys to Extraordinary* Living (with Rev. Tim Kellerman); The *Innovator's Field Guide: Accelerators for Entrepreneurs, Innovators & Change Agents; The Top Performer's Field Guide: Catalysts for Leaders, Innovators & All Who Aspire to Be;* and *Creating Startup Junkies: Building Sustainable Venture Ecosystems in Unexpected Places* (with Jeff Amerine).

In addition to his executive coaching, custom-tailored consulting, and his private equity and CEO advisory services, Jeff has received accolades for his world-class presentations, training programs, and workshops.

Jeff is an instrument-rated, multi-engine pilot; a former endurance cyclist; and has been appointed by two different governors to three separate State Boards and Commissions. Currently, he serves as a Commissioner for the Arkansas Department of Aeronautics.

Jeff and his wife Lori ("JJ and Lolo" to their two young granddaughters) make their home in Conway, Arkansas.

Special Notes

Throughout this book, we explore many examples of Grit and Grace, drawing from figures in sports, entertainment, government, and politics. While some of these individuals may evoke strong personal reactions - both positive and negative - such responses do not affect the value of their stories in illustrating the transformative power of these qualities and characteristics. This book is not about endorsing political ideologies or worldviews, nor is it intended to favor any particular perspective. Instead, its purpose is to show how the intentional pursuit of Grit and Grace can create profound personal and professional change, regardless of background, beliefs, or circumstances.

For the purposes of our discussion throughout this book, we will use common definitions for ***Leadership***, ***Grit*** (which we use synonymously with Mental Toughness and Resilience), and ***Grace*** (which we use synonymously with Emotional Intelligence and Emotional Quotient).

These definitions are as follows.

Leadership Defined

"Leadership is the most important requirement for business and personal success. In simple terms, it is defined as the willingness to be held accountable for results, and then to fulfill that responsibility, no matter what the external situation, circumstances, or pressure."

Grit (Mental Toughness and Resilience) Defined

"The quality of being adaptable, with the ability to bounce back despite significant adversity, and to remain focused on a desired outcome, regardless of the opposing forces."

Grace (Emotional Intelligence) Defined

"The ability to recognize, understand, manage, and effectively use emotions - both your own and those of others - to navigate social complexities, make thoughtful decisions, and maintain positive relationships by balancing logic with emotional insight."

Prologue

As previously mentioned, we will review multiple examples of both well-known and unknown people whose personal and professional lives have been marked by the demonstration of grit and/or grace. Our intent is to move beyond merely delivering information and to move toward facilitating transformation. As we share each example, our hope is that the reader will better understand how each quality was demonstrated, as well as the way those qualities affected each person's life. In so doing, our hope is also to make the information shared throughout this book more actionable. We start this process of example-sharing with Arkansas' own - Governor Sarah Huckabee Sanders.

Governor Sanders is no stranger to the challenges of public life. Raised in the political spotlight as the daughter of former Arkansas Governor Mike Huckabee, Sarah forged her own path through Grit and Grace, rising to become a prominent political figure in her own right. Whether one agrees with her politically or not, her journey reflects her determination to serve her state and her ability to navigate the complexities of leadership with both strength and empathy.

Growing up in a politically active family, Sanders learned about the demands of public service at an early age. Watching her father navigate the highs and lows of political life gave her a firsthand understanding of the sacrifices, challenges, and rewards involved. From an early age, she displayed a keen interest in politics, developing her own convictions and passion for public service. Her commitment to her values and convictions was shaped not only by her upbringing, but also by her deep-rooted belief in the potential of her home state and her desire to make a meaningful impact on her community.

After studying at Ouachita Baptist University, Sanders entered the world of politics, initially working on her father's presidential campaigns and later serving in various political roles, including as campaign manager and advisor for several political candidates. Her breakthrough moment came when she joined President Donald Trump's administration as White House Press Secretary. This position brought intense scrutiny, challenged her resilience, yet equipped her with invaluable experience that would later shape her leadership as the Governor of Arkansas.

Demonstrating Grit in Leadership

Grit is about unwavering commitment and the ability to endure challenges, which Sanders has demonstrated throughout her career and certainly as Governor of Arkansas. Early in her tenure, she championed the Arkansas LEARNS Act, a sweeping education reform bill that looked to overhaul the state's education system by prioritizing student-centered outcomes, expanding school choice, increasing teacher pay, and emphasizing career readiness. The act stirred considerable controversy. Facing both public and political scrutiny, Governor Sanders remained resolute in her commitment to advance this legislation. She navigated opposition on multiple fronts and endured considerable backlash from critics.

Yet, Sanders' resilience was clear as she worked tirelessly to build support for the LEARNS Act, addressing the concerns of educators, parents, and lawmakers, and emphasizing the long-term benefits for Arkansas's students and teachers. Her tenacity in pushing forward with the bill, despite these challenges, highlights her determination to improve education in Arkansas. This perseverance in the face of intense criticism and many obstacles exemplifies the core of Grit: the ability to stay committed to a vision and bring it to fruition, even when the path is challenging.

Demonstrating Grace in Leadership

Alongside Sanders' grit, her grace--her emotional intelligence--has been essential to her leadership style. Throughout her public life, she has shown the ability to manage her emotions, communicate effectively, and empathize with those she serves. During the passage of the LEARNS Act, Sanders demonstrated Grace by actively listening to the concerns of parents, teachers, and community leaders. Rather than dismissing opposing voices, she sought to understand their perspectives, inviting dialogue and constructive feedback that informed adjustments to the bill. Her commitment to listening and connecting with her constituents highlights her empathy and her desire to lead inclusively.

As governor, Sanders has prioritized connecting with Arkansans on a personal level, listening to their concerns, and attempting to understand the unique challenges faced by her constituents. Her empathy shines through in her policies and initiatives, such as the LEARNS Act, which is destined to uplift Arkansas's future generations through quality education. This approach speaks to her grace, as she navigates the complexities of leadership with humility and compassion, showing a commitment to reflecting the values and aspirations of the people she represents.

From White House to Governor's Office: The Power of Grit and Grace

Today, Governor Sanders stands as a leader who exemplifies both grit and grace. Her journey from the White House to the Arkansas governor's office reflects her dedication, resilience, and her ability to inspire others. She has demonstrated that true leadership requires both strength and empathy—the grit to persevere through challenges, as she did with the LEARNS Act, and the grace to connect meaningfully with those she serves. As governor, Sarah is committed to building a brighter future for Arkansas, drawing on her unique blend of tenacity and emotional intelligence to create lasting change in her home state.

CHAPTER ONE

The Dual Path to Excellence

"Grit without grace may win the battle, but it rarely wins the war. Grace without grit may keep the peace, but it seldom drives meaningful progress. True success, whether personal or professional, requires the delicate balance of relentless determination paired with servant leadership."

~ Jeff D. Standridge, Ed.D.

In the early 1960s, as the newly elected president of the United States, John F. Kennedy, found himself in the thick of the Cold War—a period where the fate of the world was uncertain, teetering between peace and nuclear annihilation. It was a time of intense pressure when every decision could either save or destroy millions of lives.

The Bay of Pigs invasion had just ended in a humiliating failure, shaking both his confidence and his credibility on the world stage. The media, his political opponents, and even some members of his own administration questioned his capability to lead. But as history would show, this was the crucible in which JFK's grit and grace would be forged, forever changing the course of history.

In October 1962, when U.S. intelligence discovered Soviet missiles in Cuba, Kennedy was thrust into a crisis that would test every ounce of his mental toughness and emotional intelligence. Advisers urged him to take aggressive military action, which could have triggered a nuclear war. Yet, instead of reacting with force, Kennedy displayed a rare combination of resilience and strategic calm. He knew that responding with brute strength alone could lead to catastrophic consequences, so he leaned on both mental toughness and emotional intelligence.

Kennedy's grit showed in his unwavering commitment to finding a solution, no matter how difficult it was. He worked tirelessly, sifting through conflicting advice, weighing the risks of every move, and maintaining a laser focus on the ultimate goal—resolving the crisis without bloodshed. Despite the overwhelming pressure, his vision for a bloodless resolution kept him anchored, allowing him to think clearly when others could not.

But it wasn't just his grit that mattered—it was also his grace. Kennedy's emotional intelligence was evident in his ability to connect, to gauge the intentions of his adversaries, and to navigate the tense relationships among his advisers. He knew when to be assertive and when to be empathetic, when to balance strength with resolve. During those thirteen days of the Cuban Missile Crisis, he engaged in delicate back-channel negotiations and crafted a solution that allowed both the U.S. and the Soviet Union to step back without losing face—a move that needed both toughness and empathy.

In the end, the crisis was resolved peacefully. The world breathed easier, and JFK appeared not just as a leader, but as a statesman whose legacy would be defined by his ability to blend grit with grace.

What does it take to truly excel in life, to navigate the peaks and valleys with both strength and poise? Many of us have pondered this question, particularly when faced with significant challenges or opportunities. Some say the answer lies in sheer willpower, an unyielding determination to push through adversity—what we might call Mental Toughness or Grit. Others argue that success hinges more on our ability to understand and manage emotions, to empathize with others, and to forge meaningful relationships—qualities captured in the concept of Emotional Intelligence or Grace.

But what if the key to sustained success, both personal and professional, lies not in one approach over the other, but in the delicate balance of these two forces? This book explores how the intersection of Grit and Grace can unlock a powerful pathway to excellence in every area of life. Whether you are a leader trying to inspire your team, an entrepreneur navigating the highs and lows of business, or an individual striving for personal growth, the integration of results and relationships, requiring both resilience and empathy, is essential for navigating today's complex and demanding world.

JFK, and the Cuban Missile Crisis, taught us that true success doesn't come from brute force alone, but from the mental toughness required to push forward, coupled with the emotional intelligence to understand when and how to adapt. This story is a powerful illustration of how the combination of grit and grace—mental toughness paired with emotional intelligence—can change everything, even the fate of nations. Whether you are leading a business, competing in the athletic field, or navigating life's toughest challenges, it is this balance that turns pressure into progress and adversity into achievement.

The Problem with Singular Approaches

It is tempting to think that Grit alone—the relentless drive to succeed—can carry us to the pinnacle of achievement. In fact, Grit has gained significant attention in recent years, thanks to research by psychologists such as Angela Duckworth, who showed how passion and perseverance play critical roles in long-term success. We admire the stories of people who overcame staggering odds, who outworked their competition, and who never took no for an answer. These stories resonate because they align with the belief that effort and persistence are the cornerstones of success. The life of SEAL Team SIX's Adam Brown, whom you will read about later, is such a story.

Yet, Grit without Grace often comes at a cost. In the pursuit of goals, relationships can be neglected, empathy can erode, and a narrow focus on results can lead to burnout, strained connections, and even moral compromise. We see this in the leaders who drive their teams to hit targets at the expense of well-being and trust, or in the entrepreneurs who scale businesses rapidly but lose sight of the values and relationships that sustain long-term success. Grit may get us there, but without Grace, we may find ourselves alone at the top, disillusioned or even broken.

On the flip side, Grace alone—embodied by emotional intelligence, kindness, and compassion—can also fall short if not anchored by passion and perseverance. While empathy allows us to connect deeply with others and navigate the subtleties of human relationships, an overemphasis on maintaining harmony can sometimes lead to indecision, avoidance of conflict, or a lack of accountability. In business and life, there are times when tough decisions must be made, when pushing through discomfort is the only path forward. Grace, when untethered from Grit, can result in stagnant growth, missed opportunities, and unrealized potential. While Mother Teresa certainly showed her fair share of Grit, her life is remembered for her Grace in the care for the destitute and dying in the streets of Calcutta.

Why Both Grit and Grace Matter

The truth is that both Grit and Grace are essential, not just in isolation but in their dynamic interplay. The most effective leaders, the most fulfilled individuals, and the most resilient teams understand how to wield both strength and empathy, how to push toward ambitious goals while building deep, authentic connections. This balance isn't just a nice idea—it is a strategic advantage.

Grit gives you the tenacity to keep going when circumstances are tough, to rise after failure, and to persist even when the path is uncertain. Grace, on the other hand, allows you to navigate the human elements—building trust, inspiring others, and leading with a sense of shared purpose. When fused together, these qualities create a powerful, comprehensive approach to life and leadership.

Nelson Mandela is perhaps the most universally recognized figure who exemplifies both Grit and Grace. His twenty-seven years of imprisonment for opposing apartheid tested his mental toughness and resilience; yet he exited prison, not with bitterness, but with a spirit of reconciliation and forgiveness. Mandela's grace in handling complex political and racial dynamics and his ability to unite a divided nation without resorting to revenge, showcased extraordinary emotional intelligence. He is a model of how Grit and Grace can coexist.

Consider this: In the professional world, organizations that cultivate both mental toughness/resilience (Grit) and emotional intelligence (Grace) consistently outperform those that prioritize one over the other.

Research like Google's Project Aristotle, which explored the attributes of high-performing teams, found that psychological safety—a hallmark of a team culture that embodies Grace—was the most critical factor in team success. This concept, which involves creating an environment where team members feel safe to take risks, make mistakes, and express their ideas without fear of judgment, was found to be more important than other factors, such as individual intelligence or team composition. At the same time, cultures that emphasize the elements of Grit—resilience, persistence, and a bias toward action—drive results even in uncertain environments. Collectively, these combined attributes ensure that while the team stays empathetic and open, they also drive results by being persistent and action oriented. From this, we learn that it's not a matter of choosing one over the other; it's about knowing when to lean into each quality and, more importantly, how to blend and balance them over the longer haul.

The Grit and Grace Framework

This book is organized around a simple yet powerful framework: the dual forces of Grit and Grace. These qualities—mental toughness and emotional intelligence—are essential not only for overcoming adversity but also for leading, connecting with others, and pursuing long-term goals with integrity and purpose.

Throughout these pages, we will explore what Grit and Grace mean in practical terms, how to cultivate them in your own life, and how to apply them in leadership, relationships, and personal growth. You will read stories of individuals and teams who mastered the balance between resilience and empathy, revealing both the triumphs and setbacks of their journeys.

A Personal Note on Grit and Grace

The ideas in this book are not just theoretical; they are born out of decades of experience in leadership, research, and personal growth. I have seen firsthand how the right blend of grit and grace transforms not only individuals but entire organizations and communities.

Personally, I have few problems with Grit. It comes pretty naturally to me. As a first-generation college student who began working in the third grade mowing yards, I didn't even know that "Spring Break" was a time to vacation until I was grown and had kids of my own. For me, it was just a time to work the entire week and earn money. Five days after I graduated high school, I boarded a plane where I knew no one and flew to an Army post where I knew no one and spent the next twelve weeks in one of the toughest experiences of my life—basic combat training. I worked full-time throughout my years in college, taking almost two years longer to finish than the traditional student . . . but I finished.

Soon after graduating, I bought the gas station, muffler shop, and auto service center at which I had worked from the ninth grade through my freshman year in college. I lost that business and spent the next decade paying off the debt, while working two jobs. I was no stranger to mental toughness. But, while I wasn't the proverbial A-hole, the finer points of grace, empathy, and emotional intelligence often eluded me.

Over the course of my career, there are two particular executives, incidentally, both females, whom I would call the epitomes of Grit and Grace. Multiple occurrences come to mind with each of them, but a few specific instances are etched in my memory.

Two instances occurred soon after my departure from my role as a young assistant professor to join the corporate world, in my early thirties at the time. I had been a member of this company for less than a month. Sitting in a team meeting, while the entire team was dissecting struggles of a particular project, this executive chimed in. "That was a leadership failure on my part. I let you all down there, but I will correct it, and it won't be an issue going forward." I was astonished. I had never seen a senior leader show such vulnerability and strength in a single instance.

A couple of months later, my father-in-law underwent an elective heart surgery to repair a two-decade-old coronary artery bypass. The surgery took a completely unexpected turn for the worse and he ended up in the ICU for about six weeks before he passed away. Lori and I had two young girls (five and three at the time), and she spent every day and night for six solid weeks in the ICU waiting room with her mom and sister. This same executive came to me one day, about a week into this ordeal, and said, "I know, being a newer associate, you feel like you must be here all day, every day, but I want you to go home and take care of your family. They need you. I know you'll work when you can, but I don't expect you to work when you can't. Take care of your family, first and foremost, and we'll cover you while you are out." Once again, I was completely blindsided by the degree of respect, empathy, and compassion this executive showed me so early into my tenure as one of her associates. These two instances were tremendous in shaping me as a leader.

I worked for the second executive multiple times throughout my career with the company and she showed Grit and Grace to me on a daily basis. Frequently and figuratively, she would "hold up a mirror" in front of me, allowing me to examine my behavior in a particular situation. She would question me about my words, about how I responded to a question, or how I spoke to a colleague. She would notice my emotional fluctuations and ask me how I was doing, offer her assistance, and give me guidance. In the final analysis, these two exceptional leaders forever altered the trajectory of my career by showing me, in very real terms, what it means to walk the tightrope of Grit and Grace. Oh, make no mistake about it, there were plenty of tough conversations along the way as well, but I would not be where I am today without their mentoring, coaching, guidance, and support.

Whether you are a seasoned leader, a rising professional, or someone simply seeking personal growth, these concepts are universally applicable. As you read, I encourage you to reflect on your own journey. *Where have you shown grit? Where has grace been your guiding force? And most importantly, where can you develop a deeper balance between the two?* The answers to these questions may well unlock new levels of achievement and fulfillment that you have only begun to imagine.

The Journey Ahead

The path to excellence is rarely straight or easy. It demands both resilience and compassion, as well as tenacity and empathy. In the chapters that follow, you will discover how to harness these dual forces in your own life—how to push beyond your limits while staying grounded in your values and relationships. It is not just about reaching the destination; it is about growing into the kind of person who can handle both success and setbacks with equal grace.

So, let's take this journey together. Along the way, you will learn that the road to excellence isn't a choice between grit or grace. It is about mastering both—knowing when to press forward and when to step back, when to lead with strength and when to lead with empathy. This balance, this synergy, is what makes the difference between fleeting success and lasting fulfillment.

Welcome to a life of grit and grace.

CHAPTER TWO

A Personal and Professional Journey

"There is no passion to be found playing small—in settling for a life that is less than the one you are capable of living."
~ Nelson Mandela

Envision the early 1900s, when a young reporter named Napoleon Hill was thrust into the orbit of success by a chance encounter with business titan Andrew Carnegie. The challenge bestowed upon him was monumental: he spent two decades uncovering the secrets of the most successful minds and distilling them into a recipe for others to savor. Among the ingredients in Hill's recipe, distilled from the likes of Andrew Carnegie, Henry Ford, and many others, were having a clear purpose, persistence, a pleasing personality, organized planning, and decision-making, to name a few. The resulting publication was *Think and Grow Rich*, a timeless masterpiece that echoes through the corridors of personal development even today.

Fast forward to 1982, when Jim Kouzes and Barry Posner embarked on a quest to decode the DNA of extraordinary leadership. Their findings, encapsulated in *The Leadership Challenge*, unveiled not just practices but a profound truth—leadership is not simply about having an outgoing personality or an easygoing, open communication style. Leadership is about behavior—how one behaves when leading others despite differences in age, gender, culture, or socioeconomic status.

Kouzes and Posner began their research in the early 1980s by asking thousands of people to describe their personal "best leadership experience"—a time when they felt they had performed at their peak as a leader. Through these stories, they sought to identify the common characteristics and behaviors that emerged in exceptional leadership situations. The data they collected from workshops, interviews, surveys, and case studies offered a wide range of real-world examples. Kouzes and Posner's work continues to be used by individuals and organizations all around the world.

Several years later, Stephen R. Covey's research published *The 7 Habits of Highly Effective People,* a beacon cutting through the fog of numerous personality-driven philosophies of the time. Covey's work, spanning over two hundred years of success literature, paved the way for a paradigm shift—from the fleeting allure of the Personality Ethic to the enduring strength of the Character Ethic. It is not just about how we project ourselves; it is about aligning with timeless principles and embracing the dance of character and competence.

Covey's research was built around the idea that long-lasting success and personal effectiveness are rooted in principles, not just quick techniques or situational responses. He studied the writings of influential figures, thinkers, and philosophies throughout history, including ancient Greek philosophers, religious texts, and modern psychology, to find universal, time-tested principles of human effectiveness. He drew from a wide range of leadership and management theories. He emphasized a "paradigm shift" in thinking, advocating for an inside-out approach to personal and professional effectiveness. Rather than focusing on external results or circumstances, Covey believed lasting change begins with self-awareness and alignment with principles. He became convinced that focusing on character development, rooted in universal principles (e.g., integrity, fairness, honesty), leads to enduring success, as opposed to superficial personality-based techniques that yield temporary results.

Like Kouzes and Posner's leadership practices, Covey's *7 Habits* neatly falls into the realms of self and others. Covey explains it as a dynamic connection between fostering a "private victory" within oneself, orchestrating a "public victory" in relationship with others, as well as the crucial act of "renewal" for personal growth.

My Personal Journey Unfolds

In the early 1990s, heavily influenced by these three works, I embarked on some leadership research of my own. As a young healthcare professional, I had the privilege of serving as the president of a statewide professional association at twenty-six. Barely out of college, I was thrust into this position of leadership where I readily observed vast differences in how people lead others and how they respond to leadership. I also saw that there were significant differences in the outcomes experienced by these leaders. Some consistently produced positive outcomes, while others achieved inconsistent results at best. Still, others were merely leadership figureheads. Seldom did they personally deliver consistent results, and even more rarely did they lead others to produce the same. This experience and these observations served to whet my appetite for a deeper understanding of this concept called "leadership."

At about that same time, I was appointed to the faculty of an academic health sciences center, where I served as a professor in a college that prepared allied healthcare professionals (medical technologists, radiologic technologists, genetic counselors, paramedics, respiratory therapists, etc.) for the healthcare workforce. This appointment provided me with the opportunity to study leadership as part of my official responsibilities.

Living in a rural state, our graduates often rapidly ascended the career ladder in hospitals and healthcare organizations across the state. Soon after graduating from one of our programs, it was quite common for a young professional to quickly assume a supervisory role, become a department director, or even a hospital administrator. My concern was that they had no leadership preparation to do so.

To address this gap in professional preparation, I set out to create a course for graduating seniors that would introduce them to the basic concepts of leadership, supervision, team development, performance management, and a host of other baseline leadership responsibilities. It was not long before this acquired affinity flourished into a full-blown academic and applied research interest for me.

By the mid-1990s, I had immersed myself in researching the differentiators of success for the top performers among healthcare professionals, compared to the average. More specifically, I was interested in the top 1 percent compared to the middle 50 percent.

The "Delphi" Technique is a research method established by the Rand Corporation in the 1950s. Using this method, we crafted the Respiratory Care Success Model. This model delineated the differentiating behaviors of respiratory therapists necessary to guide the profession through a tumultuous period entering the twenty-first century.

Upon reviewing this success model, the pivotal domains of self and others once again became obvious. More specifically, all the competencies identified by this research could be described as having a primary focus on self (the delivery of results), or a primary focus on others (the cultivation of relationships). For instance, the competencies of Business Orientation, Professionalism, Continuous Learning, and Self-management are commonly directed toward the individual or "self," while the competencies of Communication, Leadership, Teaming & Collaboration, and Customer Service Orientation involve behaviors that affect relationships with "others."

During my dissertation research, before reaching its final stages, I received a humbling request from senior executives at a multinational data and analytics firm, Acxiom Corporation. They wanted me to replicate my competency model research, this time focusing on the talented IT professionals within the publicly traded company. Previously, the company's job roles, performance criteria, and HR systems were solely built upon a "skills-based" model. This method presented difficulties, particularly in an era where the half-life of IT knowledge was approximately fourteen months or less. As a result of this short half-life, the skill profiles for most technical job roles became rapidly obsolete, leading to significant issues across the employee lifecycle. Although they acknowledged the necessity of finding a resolution, the specific form of any potential resolution eluded them.

Originally engaged as a consultant, I quickly made the leap from my role as a professor to deeply immerse myself in a full-time role with the company. In the years that followed, I wholeheartedly committed myself to transforming the processes and programs that govern the effectiveness of the associates and leaders within the company. This shift in approach moved away from a focus solely on the rapidly changing technical skills to a more comprehensive system centered around professional and leadership competencies.

During this time, I came across Robert E. Kelley's insightful book, *How to Be a Star at Work,* which offered valuable guidance on excelling in the workplace. Additionally, I discovered Daniel Goleman's thought-provoking work, *Working with Emotional Intelligence*, which shed a bright light on the importance of emotional intelligence in professional settings. Kelley provided a comprehensive explanation of the refined process developed at Bell Labs to uncover and confirm the unique qualities that distinguish exceptional performance in a professional setting. Once again, the range of factors that set these apart, as described by Kelley and his team, can be categorized based on their connection to oneself and their connection to others.

Goleman's book, a follow-up to his pivotal, more research-based work *Emotional Intelligence,* offered practical guidance for the development of "Personal Competence" (self) and "Social Competence" (others). Goleman offered detailed applications of emotional intelligence in the workplace and further confirmed the working hypothesis we had begun developing. Those specific observable actions or behaviors across at least two domains (self and others) are the differentiators of success between top performers and average performers. Armed with the invaluable insights gained from Goldman and Kelley, we embarked on a mission to develop a systematic approach for revealing these visible actions.

This initiative proved both exhilarating and exhausting. For eighteen months, our team worked diligently. We began by surveying all leaders and associates in the company, asking them to name the top performers across all locations. Like Kelley, we discovered considerable discrepancies between the individuals that formal company leaders identified, and those named by associates as the true top performers—a significant finding. However, after vetting each list of nominees against the others, we declared some fifty individuals, both leaders and associates, as our research group—the universally recognized top performers of the company. Our next task was to identify what differentiated these "rock stars" from the rest of the company population.

Over the next several months, we engaged each of them in extensive, recorded, behavioral-event interviews. The central question posed was: "*Tell me about a time at Acxiom when you were challenged beyond belief—when you were backed against the wall, staring into the face of failure, but you succeeded.*" Throughout the interviews, we had them describe the situation, the individuals involved, what they thought, felt, said, and finally what they actually did. The interviewer's role was to poke, prod, and probe, moving beyond the opinions of our subjects to find their actions and behaviors.

Throughout this process, we were fortunate to gather over 150 success stories—actual case studies where top performers took specific actions amid challenging situations, resulting in success. However, once the interviews concluded, our work had just begun. The task ahead involved generating written transcripts of these interviews and conducting a massive qualitative analysis to find the behaviors commonly demonstrated by our research group.

The outcome of our research, combined with earlier work, created an epiphany that began to solidify a simple yet profound model of personal and interpersonal leadership. The *Acxiom Eight*, as we referred to this model, included 37 discrete behaviors, clustered into eight competency categories, including Stakeholder Orientation, Continuous Self-directed Learning, Initiative, Results and Achievement Orientation, Planning an Organizing, Teaming and Relationship Management, Quality and Continuous Improvement, and Communication.

Once again, the behaviors defining superior performance could be categorized into two distinct domains—self and others. Behaviors involving initiative, results and achievement orientation, or planning and organizing are rooted in how we manage ourselves. On the other hand, behaviors involving stakeholder orientation, communication, teaming, and relationship management clearly involve our interaction with other people. In all cases, these exemplary behaviors were consistent across all levels of the organization. As such, these competencies became the foundation of every job role in the company, from the entry-level data analyst to the CEO. They would remain an integral part of the recruitment, selection, training, reviewing, promotion, and coaching programs for over twenty succeeding years.

Over the next two plus decades, I had the opportunity to apply, adapt, and refine this model with audiences around the world. While consistently teaching, training, and coaching in the United States, I expanded my reach to groups in the United Kingdom, France, Germany, the Netherlands, Poland, Spain, and Portugal in 2003–05. From 2005–09, I had the opportunity to work with several groups of leaders in China, Japan, and Australia. From 2010–13, I used the model with teams in the Middle East, North Africa, Latin America, and Brazil.

Since 2013, I have subjected the model to scrutiny again in the United States, working with multiple teams within various companies, institutions, and functions, including sales, operations, nonprofits, education, government, and beyond. In each instance, I refined, adapted, edited, and made improvements based on the successes, failures, and feedback from leaders and groups of functional experts.

What has become abundantly clear from years of personal experience and observation, confirmed by multiple researchers, authors, and experts, yet often left unsaid or unclarified, is that sustained individual and leadership success requires a delicate balance between two specific domains: Self and Others. Effective leaders, as well as effective individual contributors, must maintain this delicate balance between consistently managing themselves to deliver high-quality results and consciously and deliberately developing and maintaining strong, enduring relationships with those who help sustain those results.

Over the past twenty-five years, my research findings, along with those of others and my own experiences, have led me to embrace a concept that I have shared with clients and audiences across five continents. This concept asserts that: *"Effective leadership requires a delicate balance—a balance between **results** and **relationships**. Refusal to accept, understand, and honor this balance leads to failure."*

Devoting undue focus on one element, at the expense of the other, will eventually lead to suboptimal performance. An overemphasis on results, while neglecting relationships, might bring quick success, but risks alienating those crucial for sustaining those results. Conversely, an extreme focus on relationships, while overlooking results, may garner popularity initially, but lose respect when promises go unfulfilled. The scale tilts, upsetting the balance and severely affecting sustained performance.

In Stephen M.R. Covey's *The Speed of Trust*, the author delves into the profound impact of trust on individuals and organizations. Covey outlines trust's core elements: competence (results) and character (relationships). Character reflects positive qualities and ethics, guiding decisions and actions with honesty, integrity, and fairness. Competence, the ability to consistently deliver excellence, establishes credibility through technical skills and knowledge.

Covey introduces the concept of the "trust tax", highlighting the costs associated with low trust. In low-trust environments, time and energy are squandered on suspicion and resistance, thereby impeding progress. In contrast, high-trust environments boost productivity, reduce conflicts, and facilitate efficient decision-making.

In the grand scheme, sustained success and personal fulfillment require a delicate equilibrium between managing things and leading people, including oneself. This aligns with the findings from prior research, all pointing toward the same conclusion: *Success necessitates a balance across two specific domains—results and relationships*. More recently, we have refined the terminology, substituting our own references to "results" and "relationships," as well as Covey's "character" and "competence," with the terms used in this book: "Grit" and "Grace."

Grit and Grace in Action

On the surface, these two traits might seem like opposites—one hard-edged, the other soft—but they are, in fact, deeply intertwined. Together, they form a powerful combination that fuels both personal growth and professional excellence. Whether you are striving to reach the top of your field, aiming to lead a high-performing team, or simply looking to improve your life, mastering both grit and grace is essential.

The concepts of grit and grace have become central to my work as a consultant, coach, and speaker. Over the years, I have had the privilege of applying this framework in a wide variety of contexts, from helping healthcare organizations navigate change to guiding corporate leaders through complex strategic initiatives. In every instance, the principles of grit and grace have proven to be universally applicable.

For example, in leading teams through high-pressure situations—whether during the global financial crisis, organizational restructurings, or periods of rapid growth—I've found that those who succeed are not just the ones who are tough and driven. They are the ones who can inspire trust, adapt to change with humility, and maintain their integrity even under pressure. They understand that success is not just about reaching a destination but about how you get there and who you bring along with you.

One of the most impactful lessons I have learned is that the pursuit of excellence is not a zero-sum game. It is not about choosing between being results-driven or relationship-oriented. The most successful individuals and organizations integrate both approaches, using grit to stay focused and drive forward while exercising grace to engage others and keep a sense of balance and purpose. This integrated approach not only leads to better, more sustained outcomes but also fosters environments where people feel valued, respected, and motivated to do their best work.

The Path Ahead: A Journey of Grit and Grace

As we move forward in this book, you will discover that grit and grace are not just concepts but practical tools that can be developed and applied in every aspect of life. Whether you are looking to advance in your career, lead more effectively, or simply live with greater fulfillment, the integration of grit and grace will provide the foundation you need.

This chapter has outlined my personal journey and how the ideas of grit and grace evolved from research and practical application into a cohesive framework for success. The lessons I have learned—about the importance of balancing results with relationships, and the power of integrating mental toughness with emotional intelligence—led to the creation of this book.

As we explore these principles in greater depth, you will see how grit and grace are not just valuable but are transformative when practiced together. They are the keys to achieving lasting success while maintaining your humanity, integrity, and ability to connect with others. Let's embark on this journey together and discover how the synergy of grit and grace can unlock new levels of achievement, fulfillment, and growth in every area of your life.

CHAPTER THREE

Defining Grit and Grace

"It is not the strongest of the species that survive, nor the most intelligent, but the one most responsive to change."
~ Charles Darwin

The Essence of Grit

Adam Brown's life, as captured in Eric Blehm's book *Fearless: The Undaunted Courage and Ultimate Sacrifice of Navy SEAL Team SIX Operator Adam Brown*, is a testament to the power of grit, a vivid portrayal of extraordinary mental toughness and resilience that transcends the battlefield. Brown's journey is one of relentless determination, the kind of inner strength that transforms unimaginable hardships into opportunities for growth, redemption, and selfless sacrifice.

Brown's path to becoming a member of the elite SEAL Team SIX was anything but straightforward. Before donning the uniform, he was a man on the brink of losing everything, battling severe addiction that led him to hit rock bottom multiple times. For most, this would have marked the end of the road, but Brown's story is defined by his unyielding resolve to claw his way back. His decision to rebuild his life from the ashes of his past—seeking redemption, not just for himself but also for his loved ones—displays a level of grit that few possess. His mental toughness wasn't about enduring pain or hardship; it was about confronting his own demons with honesty and courage, refusing to let past failures define his future.

In the military, Brown's resilience was tested in ways that would break even the toughest of men. During a training accident, he lost the use of his dominant hand, a catastrophic injury for someone whose profession demands precise motor skills. But instead of seeing this as a roadblock, Brown saw it as a challenge. He retrained himself to shoot, fight, and operate using his non-dominant hand—a task requiring immense patience, discipline, and fortitude. And just when it seemed the odds couldn't be stacked higher against him, a battle injury stole his vision in one eye. Yet Brown's response remained the same: improvise, adapt, overcome, and continue moving forward. He refused to allow these physical limitations to dictate his capabilities, embodying the true spirit of grit—pushing beyond what others might see as impossible.

Adam Brown's ultimate test came in the unforgiving arena of combat as a member of SEAL Team SIX, one of the most demanding and dangerous units in the world. It was here that his grit truly shined, not just in his relentless drive to complete the mission, but in the grace and humility with which he carried himself. Brown's fellow operators describe him as someone who never gave less than 100 percent, even when exhaustion, pain, and the constant specter of death loomed large. His bravery under fire, his refusal to leave a teammate behind, and his unwavering dedication to his brothers in arms exemplified the kind of courage that is born from both mental toughness and an indomitable spirit.

In his final mission, Adam Brown made the ultimate sacrifice, laying down his life in the service of his country and his teammates. Even in those last moments, his actions spoke to a man driven not by fear or self-preservation, but by love, duty, and a sense of purpose larger than himself. Brown's life is a profound example of what it means to live with grit—overcoming obstacles not just for personal gain, but for the betterment of those around you.

We use the word Grit synonymously with mental toughness, resilience, and the ability to persevere through challenges. It is the quality that enables people to push through adversity, maintain focus, and stay committed to their goals despite significant setbacks. Grit is what makes the marathon runner keep going when their legs are screaming in pain, or what drives an entrepreneur to keep innovating even after multiple failures. Grit is what drove Navy SEAL Operator Adam Brown.

The Definition of Grit

Angela Duckworth, a leading researcher on grit, defines it as a combination of passion and perseverance toward long-term goals. Grit, in her view, is less about intensity and more about stamina. It's sticking with your desired future—day in, day out—not just for weeks or months, but for years, working hard to make that future a reality.

For our purposes, throughout this book, we define Grit as "***The quality of being adaptable, with the ability to bounce back despite significant adversity, and to remain focused on a desired outcome, regardless of the opposing forces.***"

But grit is more than just determination. It involves learning from failures, adapting to new circumstances, and staying focused on the ultimate goal even when the path forward drastically changes or becomes completely unclear. For those with grit, setbacks are not signals to quit but opportunities to learn and improve. They understand that the road to success is rarely smooth, and they are willing to endure discomfort, uncertainty, and disappointment if it brings them closer to their goals.

GRIT DEFINED

"The quality of being adaptable, with the ability to bounce back despite significant adversity, and to remain focused on a desired outcome, regardless of the opposing forces."

The Essence of Grace

Mother Teresa is one of the most iconic figures of grace, compassion, and emotional intelligence in modern history. Her life's work with the poorest of the poor in Calcutta and beyond serves as a profound example of what it means to live with empathy, humility, and unwavering love for humanity. Mother Teresa's approach to service was rooted in seeing the dignity and worth in every individual, no matter their condition, and responding with deep compassion and care.

Born as Anjezë Gonxhe Bojaxhiu in 1910, Mother Teresa felt a calling to devote her life to serving others from an early age. She joined the Sisters of Loreto and began her missionary work in India. However, it was in 1948 when she received what she described as a "call within a call," that her mission truly began. She left the convent to live among the poor, starting her work with the destitute and dying in the streets of Calcutta. This marked the beginning of the Missionaries of Charity, the order she founded to serve "the poorest of the poor."

Despite facing criticism and challenges, Mother Teresa remained steadfast in her mission, embodying grace through her humility. She navigated tricky situations with remarkable emotional intelligence, always choosing understanding and forgiveness over judgment. Whether addressing world leaders or tending to the dying, her ability to listen, empathize, and offer unconditional love defined her leadership and her legacy.

Her personal sacrifices and unwavering dedication to those in need illustrated that true grace is not just about kind words or gestures—it's about consistent action rooted in empathy, even when the work is difficult and the rewards are unseen. Her grace under pressure, her ability to find joy in serving the most marginalized, and her ability to forgive even those who misunderstood or criticized her are lasting testaments to her character.

Mother Teresa's impact went beyond the physical aid she provided; she gave people a sense of belonging, love, and dignity. She reminded the world that even the smallest act of kindness, done with great love, can transform lives. In a world often driven by power and competition, she stood as a beacon of humility, showing that the greatest strength lies in compassion. Her life continues to inspire people across the globe to live with grace, love unconditionally, and see the humanity in everyone.

Mother Teresa's grace was evident in her ability to connect deeply with those she served. Her emotional intelligence was reflected in her profound empathy as she not only met the physical needs of the suffering but also addressed their emotional and spiritual wounds. She treated each person with dignity, recognizing their inherent worth regardless of their circumstances. Her calm and composed demeanor, even in the face of overwhelming suffering and hardship, allowed her to bring comfort and peace to those who were often forgotten by society.

The Definition of Grace

On the other side of the coin from grit lies grace, which can be seen as the emotional intelligence needed to navigate life's challenges with empathy, self-awareness, and social understanding. Grace is what allows someone to handle difficult conversations with kindness, lead teams through crises without losing sight of human connections and remain composed under pressure. If grit is the engine that drives us forward, grace is the steering wheel that helps us navigate the road.

We use the word "Grace" synonymously with emotional intelligence, which includes self-awareness, self-regulation, empathy, motivation, and social skills. Each of these components plays a critical role in how we relate to ourselves and others. Self-awareness helps us understand our own emotions, strengths, and weaknesses. Self-regulation ensures that we respond to challenges thoughtfully rather than reacting impulsively. Empathy allows us to see situations from other perspectives and as such, connect with people on a deeper level.

A deep sense of empathy and compassion is what drove Mother Teresa to care so deeply for the destitute of Calcutta.

For our purposes throughout this book, we will define Grace as, ***"The ability to recognize, understand, manage, and effectively use emotions—both your own and those of others—to navigate social complexities, make thoughtful decisions, and maintain positive relationships by balancing logic with emotional insight."***

In leadership, grace manifests as the ability to balance firmness with compassion. Leaders who exhibit grace are not just focused on results—they prioritize relationships. They recognize that motivating a team or guiding an organization through tough times requires more than just clear directives; it requires understanding the emotions and concerns of the people involved. Graceful leaders inspire trust by listening and communicating effectively.

GRACE DEFINED

" The ability to recognize, understand, manage, and effectively use emotions—both your own and those of others—to navigate social complexities, make thoughtful decisions, and maintain positive relationships by balancing logic with emotional insight."

The Intersection of Grit and Grace

While grit and grace are powerful on their own, it is when they come together that they truly create a transformative force. The most successful people are not just determined; they are also emotionally intelligent. They know when to push forward with tenacity and when to step back in humility. They understand that achieving long-term success is not just about working hard but about working smart, leveraging both grit and grace.

Take, for example, someone who is striving to achieve a

major career milestone. Grit will keep them going through the long hours, setbacks, and moments of doubt. But without grace, they might damage relationships or become overwhelmed by stress. Grace enables them to maintain their well-being, manage relationships effectively, and lead with integrity even under intense pressure. In this way, grit and grace act as complementary forces, each enhancing the other.

In many ways, grace can be seen as the foundation that supports grit. It's grace that allows us to stay balanced in the face of stress, to manage our emotions in demanding situations, and to build and maintain positive relationships even when pursuing ambitious goals. On the other hand, grit gives us the drive to pursue those goals with unrelenting focus, even when circumstances become challenging.

Why Both Grit and Grace Are Essential

The importance of balancing grit and grace becomes clear when we consider the limitations of each quality in isolation. Grit without grace can lead to burnout, strained relationships, and a narrow focus on results at the expense of well-being. A person who is all grit may achieve their goals but at a significant personal and relational cost. By being overly fixated on the results or outcomes, they might often ignore the needs and emotions of others along the way.

Conversely, grace without grit can result in stagnation. Someone who is all grace might be well-liked and emotionally attuned but may struggle to push through difficult challenges or take decisive action when needed. He can often prioritize harmony over progress, avoiding conflict and missing opportunities for growth.

The most effective leaders and high achievers understand this balance, if not intuitively, then through experience. They know that grit without grace leads to alienation, while grace without grit leads to complacency. By integrating both grit and grace into their approach, they create an environment where challenges are met with both determination and understanding. They can push forward relentlessly while still being mindful of the needs and emotions of those around them.

The Path to Cultivating Grit and Grace

Cultivating grit and grace is a transformative journey that combines perseverance and empathy to achieve sustained success and personal fulfillment. This journey involves deliberate practice and reflection, focusing on building habits that reinforce resilience and emotional awareness. Whether your natural tendency leans toward grit or grace (and we all have natural tendencies toward one or the other), this path begins with self-awareness—understanding your strengths, weaknesses, motivations, and values. From there, the focus is on developing balanced habits that strengthen both your resolve and your relationships.

Developing a Growth Mindset

A growth mindset is the foundation for building both grit and grace. Popularized by psychologist Carol Dweck, a growth mindset is the belief that abilities, intelligence, and talents can be developed through effort, learning, and persistence. In contrast to a fixed mindset—which assumes that our capabilities are static—a growth mindset views challenges as opportunities for growth rather than threats.

To cultivate a growth mindset, start by embracing setbacks and failures as learning experiences. Reflect on mistakes to understand what went wrong and identify actionable steps for improvement. Remind yourself that effort and practice are the primary paths to growth. Surround yourself with people who encourage learning and embrace constructive feedback, as this environment fosters the resilience and openness necessary for personal development. By adopting a growth mindset, you will set the stage for lifelong learning and build the mental flexibility to handle challenges with grit and grace.

The Power of Synergy

As we have shown, the interplay between grit and grace is where the real magic happens. It is what allows us to pursue big dreams while staying grounded, to overcome adversity without losing our humanity, and to lead others with both strength and compassion. Whether in business, personal relationships, or self-development, mastering this balance is the key to long-term success and fulfillment.

Building grit and grace is like training both strength and flexibility in the body—they complement each other and are essential for balanced growth. Just as athletes strengthen their physical endurance, individuals can train their minds and emotions through deliberate practice and reflection. This holistic approach to personal development creates a balanced foundation where mental toughness and emotional intelligence work in tandem.

By consistently working on both grit and grace, you will be better prepared to handle life's challenges with resilience, adapt gracefully to change, and connect deeply with others. True excellence doesn't come from toughness alone or emotional awareness alone; it comes from integrating these qualities and nurturing both mental resilience and compassionate empathy.

As you continue through this book, you will more deeply explore how grit and grace can be applied in various aspects of life—from leadership to personal growth—and how you can cultivate these qualities in yourself. Remember, the goal is not to choose one over the other but to develop both in harmony. By doing so, you'll be equipped to navigate any challenge with resilience, empathy, and integrity, setting the stage for a life marked by both achievement and connection.

In the chapters ahead, you will discover practical strategies for integrating grit and grace into your daily life, learn from inspiring stories of individuals who have embodied these qualities, and gain insights that will empower you to reach your highest potential.

CHAPTER FOUR

A Deeper Look at Grit

"Success is not final; failure is not fatal. It is the courage to continue that counts."

~ Winston Churchill

Elon Musk, a name synonymous with audacity and innovation, stands as living evidence of the embodiment of mental toughness. Born in Pretoria, South Africa, in 1971, Musk displayed an early proclivity for technology and entrepreneurship. His dedicated pursuit of ambitious goals and steadfast resilience through multiple setbacks paints a vivid picture of what it truly means to embody grit.

Musk's journey into the world of entrepreneurship started early. In his youth, he displayed an insatiable curiosity, devouring books and exploring the fields of science and technology. After completing his studies at the University of Pretoria, he set his sights on the United States, driven by a fervent desire to make an impact on the world.

In 1995, Musk embarked on his first entrepreneurial venture with Zip2, a city guide software for newspapers. The road was fraught with challenges as Musk faced many rejections from potential investors. The grit to persist in the face of adversity defined this early chapter of his career. Despite the setbacks, Musk's determination prevailed, and Compaq acquired Zip2 in 1999, laying the foundation for Musk's future endeavors.

After the sale of Zip2, Musk co-founded X.com, an online payment company. Despite achieving initial success, internal conflicts and external challenges led to Musk's departure from X.com. However, rather than succumbing to these setbacks, he doubled down on his vision. In 2002, X.com merged with Confinity to become what we now know as PayPal. Under Musk's leadership, PayPal became a trailblazer in online payment systems. In 2002, eBay bought PayPal for $1.5 billion. Musk's journey at PayPal displayed the resilience and adaptability that define grit. The ability to bounce back from adversity and transform challenges into opportunities became a recurring theme in Musk's narrative.

While many would have considered achieving success in the online payment industry a significant accomplishment, Musk's aspirations soared even higher—literally. In 2002, he founded SpaceX with a bold vision of making life multi-planetary. This audacious goal was met with skepticism and cynicism from the aerospace industry. Undeterred, Musk poured his own funds into SpaceX, overcoming multiple failures in the early attempts to launch rockets.

The breakthrough came in 2008, when SpaceX successfully launched the Falcon 1, becoming the first privately funded, liquid-fueled rocket to reach orbit. This achievement marked a paradigm shift in space exploration and solidified Musk's reputation as a visionary leader with an unyielding determination to turn dreams into reality.

Amid SpaceX's triumphs, Musk set his sights on yet another audacious endeavor—revolutionizing the automotive industry. With the founding of Tesla Motors in 2003, Musk aimed to accelerate the world's transition to sustainable energy. The road was rocky, with financial challenges, production woes, and skepticism from the automotive establishment.

He faced personal and professional strains, often working grueling hours and investing a sizable portion of his own fortune to keep Tesla afloat. The pivotal moment came with the launch of the Tesla Roadster in 2008, showcasing the viability of electric vehicles. Tesla, against all odds, became a symbol of innovation and sustainability, fueled by Musk's grit and unrelenting stamina.

Musk's journey extends beyond SpaceX and Tesla,

encompassing ventures such as SolarCity, a solar energy services company; Neuralink, focused on neural technology; and The Boring Company, aiming to revolutionize tunnel construction. Each venture brought its set of challenges and doubters, but Musk's resilience and grit remained unwavering.

Through turbulent financial periods, technical hurdles, and public scrutiny, Musk's ability to persevere, adapt, and thrive against the odds has been a recurring theme. His leadership style, marked by an unrelenting pursuit of ambitious goals, has redefined industries and inspired a new generation of entrepreneurs.

Grit Under Siege

A recent study of several thousand subjects, including employees from multiple organizations, found only a small percentage of subjects to be mentally resilient. Several other researchers have found that employees in organizations worldwide increasingly lack a baseline level of grit. The following paints the picture:

- According to the American Psychological Association, burnout and stress are at all-time highs across multiple professions and among healthcare workers.
- In 2021, American workers saw heightened rates of burnout, with 79 percent reporting some degree of work-related stress in the month immediately preceding the "Work and Well-being Survey".
- Three in five employees reported being negatively affected by work-related stress, including lack of interest, motivation, or energy (26 percent), lack of effort at work (19 percent), cognitive weariness (36 percent), emotional exhaustion (32 percent), and physical fatigue (44 percent).
- According to Gallup, around one-third of individuals worldwide reported feeling angry, worried, and stressed, and one in four workers experienced burnout either "always" or "very often."
- Finally, the Mental Health Foundation reported that 74

percent of individuals had experienced stress to the level that they were unable to address or cope with it.

The Impact of Grit

Developing even a modicum of grit prepares us to be the best versions of ourselves, despite the challenges we face from day to day. It helps us sustain our efforts, persevere through discomfort, rebound from temporary setbacks, as well as achieve and sustain peak performance across multiple areas of our lives.

In sports, athletes who have mental toughness are highly likely to produce favorable performance outcomes in ways that promote sustained motivation. For example, golfers with higher levels of motivation have lower levels of anxiety. So, motivation and mental toughness tend to be tightly linked, leading not only to positive results, but also to reduced anxiety, and emotional strength and stability.

Being mentally tough not only improves our personal and professional lives, but it also brings many benefits to organizations. According to Mental Toughness Partners, research conducted throughout the world found that people with better and higher levels of mental toughness, as measured by the MTQ48, tend to enjoy many benefits, including the following:

- **Increased aspirations:** Greater confidence and ambition in the pursuit of defined goals, as well as a stronger willingness to persevere.
- **Adaptability to change:** A lower and calmer stress response to unanticipated changes.
- **Greater well-being:** Improved stress management and higher levels of contentment.
- **Improved positivity:** Connectivity and rapport with colleagues due to a can-do attitude.
- **Better performance:** Accounting for up to 25 percent of variations in organizational performances.

As you can see, grit is a key ingredient in achieving long-term success. It is the inner strength that allows you to persevere in the face of adversity, maintain focus on your goals, and bounce back from setbacks stronger than before. Grit is not just about having passion; it's about sustaining that passion over the long haul, even when the road gets rough. This chapter dives into the core elements of grit, how they can be cultivated, and why they are critical to both personal and professional success.

The Core Components of Grit

Mental toughness is a multifaceted construct, encompassing several key attributes that contribute to resilience and perseverance. Let's explore the main components:

RESILIENCE: Resilience is the ability to recover from setbacks and adapt to troublesome situations. It is a critical factor that differentiates those who succeed from those who throw in the towel when the path gets rocky. Research consistently shows that resilience not only improves well-being but also plays a significant role in performance and success across different fields. Resilient individuals are more likely to remain committed to their goals despite facing obstacles. Studies in both educational and workplace settings demonstrate that individuals with high resilience report higher job satisfaction and are more engaged in their work.

PERSEVERANCE: Perseverance is the determination to keep going despite challenges or failures. It is not just about working hard in the short term; it's also about staying committed over time. Angela Duckworth's research on grit shows that perseverance is often a more reliable predictor of success than talent. Those who persevere tend to achieve more in the long run because they are willing to push through difficulties and remain focused on their goals.

PASSION: While perseverance is about sticking with something, passion is what keeps the flame burning. Passion drives people to keep moving forward, even when the going gets tough. Passionate individuals are not just interested in their goals; they are deeply committed to them, which fuels their persistence over time. Passion is the spark that ignites mental toughness, and it is essential for sustaining long-term efforts.

COURAGE: Courage is the ability (and willingness) to take thoughtful risks and face challenges, even when there is uncertainty. Courage is not the absence of fear; it's acting decisively despite being fearful. In the context of mental toughness, courage is the willingness to step out of your comfort zone, embrace challenges, and keep pushing forward, even when there is no guarantee of success. Leaders and innovators who demonstrate courage are often the ones who achieve groundbreaking success.

SELF-DISCIPLINE: Mental toughness requires a high degree of self-discipline—the ability to stay focused and resist distractions. Self-discipline is what keeps you on track day after day, even when motivation wanes. It's the discipline to follow through on commitments, maintain good habits, and push yourself even when you don't feel like it. Without self-discipline, grit will falter under pressure.

Forging Unbreakable Grit

The good news is that mental toughness is not something you are simply born with—it can be developed and strengthened over time. If you are ready to dig deeply, here are some strategies for cultivating grit so you don't just survive the storms of life, but you thrive in them.

1. **Commit to a Relentless Growth Mindset:** Developing grit means embracing a mindset that doesn't flinch at obstacles. With a growth mindset, every failure becomes fuel, every setback a lesson. This isn't about being positive—it's about rejecting limits. Mentally tough people look at challenges and say, "I'm here to learn, adapt, and conquer." Commit to seeing struggle as part of the climb. When you lock into growth, you are choosing resilience, progress, and the relentless pursuit of becoming stronger with every battle you face.
2. **Set Ambitious Goals and See Them Through:** If you want grit, you need goals that pull you forward, even when the going gets brutal. Goals aren't just benchmarks; they are battle plans that keep you fighting. Add visualization, and you're not just setting a target—you're living it. Imagine every detail, every move, every win. Top athletes, unstoppable leaders, and those who refuse to quit use this to hardwire confidence and readiness.
3. **Embrace Failure and Use It as Fuel:** Failure is coming, but it is not the end. It is the beginning. Mentally tough people don't just face failure—they dissect it, own it, and use it as fuel to go harder. If you are serious about building resilience, adopt a growth mindset. Failures? They are just steppingstones to your next comeback.
4. **Build Your Stress Armor:** Stress inoculation training (SIT) is about training in the fire before the fire comes. It is controlled exposure to pressure—building resistance in a way that makes high-stakes moments feel like just another drill. Whether through guided training or by facing your stressors head-on, you will condition yourself to stay calm, focused, and deadly effective in the heat of any moment.
5. **Win the Battle Between Your Ears:** When things get tough, your inner voice better be tougher. Positive

self-talk isn't fluff; it is ammunition. Replace every self-doubt with an affirmation of your strength and capability. Build a habit of saying, "I've got this," and you will hardwire your mind to withstand anything.

6. **Rely on a Powerful Support Squad:** True grit isn't always a solo journey. Those who weather the fiercest storms often have a strong crew backing them up. Family, friends, mentors—they are your safety net and your boost. Surround yourself with those who push you, who ground you, and who will not let you quit. It's not just about staying resilient—it is about having allies who will stand shoulder to shoulder with you when it counts.

Grit-Related Habits: Building Mental Toughness

To strengthen grit, focus on habits that reinforce resilience, determination, and goal setting. These habits encourage you to push through discomfort, work toward long-term goals, and stay disciplined in the face of adversity.

- **Set Meaningful Long-Term Goals**: Define goals that align with your core values and passions, such as in areas like health, career, relationships, and personal growth. When goals are meaningful to you, you are more likely to stay committed.
- **Break Goals into Manageable Steps**: Break down long-term goals into small, achievable steps. By creating milestones, you build momentum and reinforce a sense of accomplishment, making it easier to stay on course.
- **Implement Consistent Daily Habits**: Consistency is key to grit. Establish daily habits that move you closer to your goals, even if they are small steps. Whether it is a daily exercise routine, a regular study schedule, or a budgeting practice, these actions create a foundation of discipline.

- **Embrace Discomfort and Self-Discipline**: Mental toughness is built by doing things that are challenging but beneficial. Adopt habits like regular exercise, maintaining a balanced diet, practicing financial discipline, and facing uncomfortable conversations head-on. These habits reinforce your ability to handle adversity.
- **Practice Resilience by Reframing Challenges**: View challenges as opportunities for growth rather than obstacles. When setbacks occur, remind yourself that adversity is a chance to strengthen your skills and resilience. Embrace challenges with the mindset of "what can I learn from this?" to foster mental toughness.

Real-World Examples of Grit

Mental toughness is not an abstract concept—it manifests in the stories of people who have faced significant challenges and persevered against the odds. Let's look at a few more examples:

Malala Yousafzai – Education Activist and Nobel Laureate: In 2012, at the age of 15, Yousafzai was shot in the head by the Taliban for advocating for girls' education in Pakistan. She survived the attack and underwent extensive surgeries and rehabilitation. Instead of retreating, Malala used her near-death experience to further champion the cause of girls' education on a global scale. She became the youngest recipient of the Nobel Peace Prize in 2014 and continues to advocate for education despite the personal dangers. Her resilience in the face of violence and her relentless pursuit of justice makes her an outstanding example of grit.

Alex Honnold – Professional Rock Climber: Honnold is best known for his free solo climb of El Capitan in Yosemite National Park, a 3,000-foot vertical rock face, without ropes or safety equipment in 2017. The climb was widely regarded as one of the most dangerous feats in climbing history, where a single mistake could result in death. Honnold's mental resilience was critical as he meticulously planned and practiced every move over the course of several years. His ability to maintain focus, control his fear, and push the limits of human physical and mental capacity showed an extraordinary level of mental toughness.

David Goggins – Former Navy SEAL and Ultra-Endurance Athlete: Goggins grew up in an abusive household, struggled with obesity, and faced learning disabilities. He eventually joined the military but initially failed in his attempts to become a Navy SEAL. He also faced significant physical challenges, including undergoing multiple surgeries. Despite these obstacles, Goggins became a Navy SEAL, an Army Ranger, and one of the world's toughest endurance athletes. He completed ultra-marathons, triathlons, and set a world record for pull-ups. His philosophy of embracing pain and pushing beyond perceived limits made him a modern symbol of mental toughness and resilience.

Simone Biles – Olympic Gymnast: Simone Biles is considered one of the greatest gymnasts of all time. However, during the 2021 Tokyo Olympics, she faced an immense mental health struggle known as "the twisties," a dangerous condition in which gymnasts lose control of their sense of spatial awareness mid-air. Biles made the difficult decision to withdraw from several events to prioritize her mental health—a decision that sparked a global conversation about the importance of mental resilience. She returned to compete in the balance beam final, winning a bronze medal. Her openness about mental health challenges, combined with her ability to refocus and persevere under pressure, redefined what grit looks like in elite athletes.

Bethany Hamilton – Professional Surfer: Hamilton lost her left arm in a shark attack at age 13 while surfing off the coast of Hawaii. The attack could have ended her surfing career and drastically altered her life. Despite this traumatic event, Hamilton returned to competitive surfing just a few months after the attack and continued to compete at a professional level. Hamilton's journey of adapting to her new circumstances and continuing to pursue her goals despite physical limitations is a shining example of mental toughness. Her story has inspired millions and proves how grit can help us overcome even the most devastating setbacks.

Wilma Rudolph – Olympic Gold Medalist: Rudolph overcame significant physical challenges to become the first American woman to win three gold medals in a single Olympic Games. Born prematurely and later contracting polio, Rudolph was told she would never walk again without braces. Yet, through sheer determination, she not only learned to walk but also became one of the fastest women in the world. Her story highlights the power of resilience and courage in the face of seemingly insurmountable odds.

The Power of Grit in Your Journey

Mental toughness is not just for elite athletes or high-powered executives; it is a quality that everyone can develop to enhance their personal and professional lives. By cultivating resilience, perseverance, passion, and courage, you can build the grit needed to overcome obstacles and achieve your long-term goals. The strategies discussed in this chapter—setting clear goals, embracing failure, practicing positive self-talk, and building powerful support networks—are all actionable steps that can help you develop greater mental toughness.

As you continue your journey, remember that grit is not about never falling—it is about getting back up every time you do. It's about pushing forward even when the path is unclear and having the courage to stay committed to your vision. By integrating these principles into your daily life, you will be better equipped to face challenges with resilience and determination, leading to greater success and fulfillment.

CHAPTER FIVE

A Deeper Look at Grace

"When dealing with people, remember you are not dealing with creatures of logic, but creatures of emotion."
~ Dale Carnegie

In the high-pressure world of professional sports, where the spotlight shines brightly and the stakes are always sky-high, it can be easy for athletes to become consumed by their own egos and the constant drive for victory. It is the rare individual who can transcend the constant demands and find a way to succeed, not just through sheer talent and skill, but through a deeper understanding of themselves and those around them. One such athlete is Stephen Curry; the superstar point guard for the Golden State Warriors

Curry's path to NBA superstardom has been anything but conventional. As the son of former NBA player Dell Curry, he grew up in the shadow of his father's success, constantly working to prove that he was more than just a famous name. Despite his prodigious shooting ability from a young age, Curry was often overlooked and underestimated, with scouts and analysts questioning whether his slight frame and unorthodox playing style would translate to the professional level.

However, Curry's journey to the top of the NBA was defined, not just by his basketball skills, but also by his unwavering dedication, his humble demeanor, and his remarkable emotional intelligence. From the very beginning of his career, Curry has been known for his team-first mentality, his willingness to sacrifice individual glory for the greater good of his squad, and his ability to connect with his teammates and coaching staff on a deep, personal level.

This was most evident during the 2015–2016 season, when Curry led the Warriors to a historic 73–9 record, surpassing the earlier mark set by the 1995–1996 Chicago Bulls. Amid this incredible run, Curry could have easily allowed his individual success to inflate his ego and distance himself from his teammates. Instead, he stayed firmly grounded, constantly praising the contributions of his fellow players and crediting the team's chemistry and companionship as the driving force behind their historic campaign.

Off the court, Curry's emotional intelligence has been equally impressive. Despite the immense pressure and scrutiny that comes with being a global superstar, he has consistently shown a remarkable level of composure and poise, never letting the outside noise or the demands of fame distract him from his true passions and priorities.

One of the clearest examples of Curry's emotional intelligence came during the 2016 NBA Finals when the Warriors found themselves trailing the Cleveland Cavaliers 3–1 in the series. In the face of this daunting deficit, Curry could have easily fallen into despair or allowed the pressure to get the better of him. Instead, he rallied his teammates, preaching the importance of staying positive and focused and reminding them of all the work they had put in to reach this point.

Curry's unwavering faith and positive attitude proved to be the difference-maker, as the Warriors stormed back to win the next three games and claim their second NBA championship in franchise history. In the aftermath of the victory, Curry's gracious and humble demeanor was on full display as he repeatedly praised his teammates and coaching staff and expressed his gratitude for the support of the Warriors' loyal fanbase.

This same approach has defined Curry's entire career, as he has consistently used his platform to uplift and empower those around him. Whether he is mentoring young players, using his voice to promote social justice and community development, or simply taking the time to connect with his fans, Curry has always shown a deep understanding of the impact that his actions can have on others.

One particularly poignant example of Curry's emotional intelligence and grace came in the wake of the COVID-19 pandemic, which brought the entire world to a standstill and forced the NBA to suspend its season. Rather than retreating into isolation or focusing solely on his own well-being, Curry sprang into action at once, using his vast network and resources to support those most affected by the crisis.

From organizing virtual workout sessions to keep his teammates and fans engaged to partnering with local organizations to provide meals and essential supplies to those in need, Curry demonstrated a remarkable level of empathy and compassion. He understood that in times of crisis, the true measure of a leader is not just his ability to perform on the court but his willingness to use their platform to uplift and support his community.

This sense of responsibility and concern for others has been a consistent thread throughout Curry's career, and it has earned him the respect and admiration of not just his peers but fans and observers around the world. In a landscape where so many athletes are driven by ego and the pursuit of individual glory, Curry stands out as a shining example of what can be achieved when emotional intelligence and grace are combined with exceptional talent and skills.

Grace Under Fire

While emotional intelligence, also referred to as emotional quotient (EQ), plays a critical role in mental resilience, social adaptability, and workplace success, recent studies show that our collective capacity for emotional intelligence is diminishing, with significant impacts on well-being, productivity, and organizational culture.

- A 2021 study revealed that 63 percent of physicians reported symptoms of burnout, and only 30 percent felt satisfied with their work-life balance. Rates of burnout across the entire healthcare industry exceed 40 percent among clinicians, and in some groups, approaches 80 percent. Burnout is now prevalent across every industry worldwide. Emotional intelligence, which includes skills such as empathy, self-awareness, and emotional regulation, has been shown to reduce burnout, improve resilience, and enhance overall job performance; but many workers struggle to develop and sustain these skills.
- Another global study found that EQ and well-being have declined steadily over the past several years, correlating with increased burnout and decreased job satisfaction.
- A cross-temporal meta-analysis of seventy studies involving 17,000 participants found significant declines in three facets of EQ: well-being, self-control, and emotional self-regulation. The analysis highlighted that these societal changes, including the rise of social media and reduced in-person interactions, are correlated with these declines. The study concluded that these trends could contribute to increased loneliness, depression, and anxiety in younger generations.
- The State of the Heart Report, conducted by Six Seconds (an emotional intelligence non-profit research organization), revealed that global emotional intelligence scores have been on a consistent decline for the past four years, with an overall decrease of 5.54 percent in emotional intelligence competencies. This decline has contributed to what the report describes as an "emotional recession," characterized by decreased well-being, reduced empathy, and higher burnout levels, especially in younger generations.
- Recent research conducted by management consulting firm Korn Ferry, which included a global sample of 10,000 people, found significant declines in emotional self-regulation and self-awareness. These findings are

linked to the growing challenges of maintaining in-person relationships and the psychological effects of prolonged remote work during and after the pandemic.

These studies suggest that the decline in emotional intelligence is a global issue, affecting both personal and professional spheres. The implications of these findings are profound, indicating that emotional intelligence training and interventions may become increasingly critical to addressing mental health and social well-being.

The Impact of Grace

Developing grace/EQ provides significant benefits across various aspects of our personal and professional lives, much like grit and mental toughness. The ability to understand, manage, and effectively utilize emotions is crucial for achieving both personal well-being, relational longevity, and professional success.

Multiple experts have demonstrated the positive impact of emotional intelligence, including the following:

- **Improved Interpersonal Relationships:** EQ enhances the quality of relationships by fostering better communication, empathy, and conflict resolution skills. People with high EQ are more adept at navigating social complexities, which leads to stronger and more meaningful connections both at home and in the workplace.

- **Enhanced Leadership and Performance:** Research indicates that leaders with high EQ are more effective, capable of motivating their teams, and are better at fostering positive organizational cultures. Such leaders are also more resilient in the face of challenges and better equipped to manage stress, which translates to improved organizational performance and employee satisfaction.

- **Better Mental Health and Well-being:** High EQ is linked to lower levels of anxiety and depression. Individuals with strong EQ are more resilient to stress and are better at regulating their emotions, leading to improved overall well-being. They are less likely to experience burnout and are more capable of keeping a positive outlook in the face of adversity.

- **Increased Motivation and Productivity:** EQ contributes to sustained motivation by helping individuals align their goals with their values and maintain their focus. This alignment reduces procrastination and fosters intrinsic motivation, leading to higher levels of productivity and goal achievement.

- **Adaptability and Problem-solving:** Emotionally intelligent individuals are better at adapting to change and handling uncertainty. Their ability to remain calm and assess situations rationally allows them to make better decisions, even under pressure. This adaptability makes them valuable assets in dynamic environments.

One might think that the term Grace is a bit too narrow to be used synonymously with the concept of EQ; however, a review of synonyms supports our decision in that regard. Terms such as self-assurance, composure, empathy, and respect, among others, don't exactly describe the elements of Grace, but they certainly point to the product.

SYNONYMS FOR "GRACE"

Self-assurance
Composure
Dignity
Refinement
Empathy
Gentleness
Respect
Politeness

The Core Components of Grace

Emotional intelligence is commonly broken down into five key components: self-awareness, self-regulation, motivation, empathy, and social skills. Each plays a unique role in fostering grace, and together they form the foundation of emotionally intelligent behavior.

Self-Awareness: Self-awareness is the cornerstone of EQ. It involves having a clear understanding of one's own emotions, strengths, weaknesses, values, and motivations. Self-aware individuals are in tune with their inner emotional landscape, allowing them to navigate life with greater clarity and intentionality.

Cultivating self-awareness requires regular introspection and a willingness to examine one's thoughts, feelings, and behaviors. Practices such as mindfulness, journaling, and reflective questioning can deepen self-awareness and provide valuable insights into how emotions influence decision-making. Feedback from others also plays a critical role in enhancing self-awareness by offering perspectives that may be overlooked during self-reflection.

Self-Regulation: Self-regulation is the ability to manage and control emotional impulses, which is essential for maintaining composure and making rational decisions under pressure. This skill allows individuals to pause, reflect, and choose their responses rather than reacting impulsively. Effective self-regulation involves managing negative emotions, embracing flexibility in challenging situations, and maintaining integrity even when it is difficult.

Developing self-regulation requires practicing techniques such as cognitive-behavioral strategies, emotion regulation exercises, and stress management approaches. By enhancing self-regulation, individuals can better navigate high-stakes environments, reduce conflict, and foster more positive interactions.

Motivation: Motivation in the context of EQ goes beyond external rewards. It refers to the intrinsic drive to pursue goals with energy and persistence. Emotionally intelligent individuals are often self-motivated and derive satisfaction from personal growth, progress, and the pursuit of purpose. They maintain a hopeful outlook even in the face of setbacks, seeing challenges as opportunities rather than obstacles.

Strategies for enhancing motivation include setting meaningful goals, celebrating small wins, and maintaining a positive mindset through visualization and self-affirmation. Emotionally intelligent individuals often strike a balance between striving for achievement and staying grounded in their values.

Empathy: Empathy is the ability to understand and share the feelings of others. It involves recognizing emotional cues, appreciating diverse perspectives, and responding with compassion. Unlike sympathy, which is more about feeling sorry for someone, empathy requires deeper emotional engagement and the ability to connect by understanding how they feel.

Developing empathy involves active listening, perspective-taking, and engaging with diverse experiences. By practicing empathy, individuals can build stronger relationships, resolve conflicts more effectively, and create environments where people feel valued and understood.

Social Skills: Social skills are the abilities that allow individuals to communicate effectively, build relationships, and navigate social networks. These skills include conflict resolution, teamwork, and the capacity to inspire and influence others. Strong social skills are essential for leaders and anyone who interacts with others regularly.

Developing social skills requires consistent practice, including engaging in active listening, practicing effective communication techniques, and learning how to manage and resolve conflicts constructively. Emotionally intelligent individuals use these skills to create harmonious relationships, foster collaboration, and lead with influence and respect.

Forging Unshakable Grace

Just like grit, grace is not something that everyone is naturally born with—but it can be developed and strengthened over time. To cultivate real grace, you must work at it, just like building muscle. Here's how to become someone who stays steady, composed, and connected, no matter what comes your way.

1. **Master Introspection and Mindfulness:** Real grace starts with self-awareness. Get serious about mindfulness practices—whether it is meditation, reflection, or journaling. These routines aren't about calmness; they are about building mental space between you and your triggers, so you can respond with purpose, not react out of impulse. Know yourself deeply, and you will own your emotions instead of being owned by them.
2. **Listen Like Your Life Depends on It:** Grace isn't just about you; it is about how you connect with others. Active listening—really tuning in without planning your next move—can reshape how you interact. Add perspective-taking, and you are intentionally stepping into someone else's world. When you listen

to understand, you're not just hearing words; you are building the kind of empathy that powers authentic, graceful responses.

3. **Seek Unfiltered Feedback and Constantly Level Up:** True growth requires brutal honesty. Regularly seek feedback from people who will tell you the hard truths. This feedback shines a light on blind spots and gives you a path to continuous improvement. Grace is a skill that demands practice and learning from both triumphs and setbacks.
4. **Use Emotional Control as Your Edge:** Grace under pressure means staying cool when others would crumble. Use techniques like deep breathing, cognitive reframing, and sharp self-talk to control intense emotions. Practicing these daily will build a core of calm so solid that even high-pressure moments won't shake you. It is not just about control—it's about commanding your inner world.
5. **Go All in on Empathy:** Grace connects us all, and empathy is its core. Push yourself to understand others on a deeper level—whether through volunteering, reading diverse stories, or actively seeking out new perspectives. These exercises broaden your understanding of what people go through and deepen your connections. Real grace isn't about kindness; it's about understanding.

Grace-Related Habits: Developing Emotional Intelligence

Grace is cultivated by nurturing self-awareness, empathy, and positive relationships. These habits help you become more emotionally intelligent and improve your ability to manage stress, connect with others, and navigate complex social situations.

- **Engage in Self-Reflection**: Regularly take time to reflect on your emotions, triggers, and reactions. Journaling or using mindfulness techniques can help you become more aware of your behavioral patterns and responses to different situations, which is essential for personal growth.
- **Practice Empathic Listening**: Show genuine interest in others' perspectives by listening without judgment or interruption. Ask open-ended questions, validate others' feelings, and strive to understand their point of view. This practice strengthens relationships and enhances emotional intelligence.
- **Practice Emotional Regulation**: Use mindfulness techniques, such as deep breathing or meditation, to help you stay calm in stressful situations. By cultivating awareness of your emotional state, you will be better equipped to respond thoughtfully instead of reacting impulsively.
- **Build Trusting Relationships**: Develop connections that are rooted in trust, respect, and mutual support. Invest in people who encourage your growth, support your well-being, and challenge you to be your best self. Healthy relationships foster a sense of belonging and emotional stability.

Real-World Examples of Grace

While a mental toughness is more concrete in its manifestation, emotional intelligence can be more abstract. But like mental toughness, it manifests in the stories of people who demonstrate self-awareness, self-regulation, empathy, motivation, and social skills. The following examples illustrate how these qualities have been displayed in different circumstances.

Satya Nadella – CEO of Microsoft: When Nadella became CEO of Microsoft in 2014, the company was facing challenges in staying relevant in a rapidly changing tech landscape.

Nadella led a cultural shift within the company, moving from a competitive, insular mindset to one focused on collaboration and empathy. Nadella's approach centered on empathy, which he personally cultivated as the father of a son with cerebral palsy. His leadership style emphasized listening, inclusiveness, and emotional sensitivity to employees' needs, which helped reshape Microsoft's culture and made it a more innovative and compassionate workplace. His ability to connect with employees and foster a more emotionally intelligent company culture contributed to Microsoft's resurgence under his leadership.

Tim Cook – CEO of Apple: After succeeding Steve Jobs as CEO of Apple in 2011, Cook was tasked with leading one of the world's most successful companies through a period of transition. Cook had the difficult challenge of following in the footsteps of a visionary leader and maintaining Apple's creative legacy. Cook demonstrated tremendous emotional intelligence by maintaining his own authentic leadership style rather than mimicking Jobs'. He focused on fostering a more inclusive and transparent company culture, where diversity and social responsibility were emphasized. His ability to listen, engage in open dialogue with employees, and prioritize ethical decisions, such as standing up for customer privacy, has shown how emotional intelligence can help sustain innovation and moral leadership in a tech giant.

Amanda Gorman – Poet and Activist: Amanda Gorman captured the world's attention when she became the youngest inaugural poet in U.S. history at 22, performing *The Hill We Climb*, at President Joe Biden's inauguration in 2021. Her poem and delivery addressed themes of hope, unity, and resilience in a divided nation. Gorman's emotional intelligence shines through her poetry and public presence. She uses her art to empathize with others' struggles while offering hope and a vision for the future. Despite struggling with a speech impediment as a child,

Gorman developed self-confidence and embraced vulnerability, demonstrating resilience and self-regulation. Her ability to convey profound emotion and connect with diverse audiences through her words speaks to her emotional awareness and empathy, making her a powerful voice for social justice and change.

Marcus Rashford – Professional Soccer Player and Philanthropist: Marcus Rashford, a professional soccer player for Manchester United and the England national team, grew up in a low-income family. During the COVID-19 pandemic, he spearheaded a campaign to ensure children in the UK had access to free school meals when schools were closed. Despite being a young athlete, Rashford used his platform to address childhood hunger. Rashford showed elevated levels of empathy and social awareness by understanding the struggles of disadvantaged families, reflecting his own experiences growing up. His communication skills allowed him to influence policymakers, leading to government action on the issue. Rashford's ability to use his platform for social good while maintaining humility and resilience, even when facing challenges on the field, highlights his strong emotional intelligence.

Applications of Grace

The principles of emotional intelligence are not just theoretical—they have real-world applications across various contexts:

Leadership

Emotionally intelligent leaders create cultures of trust, respect, and high performance. They are attuned to the emotional needs of their team members and know how to motivate, inspire, and resolve conflicts. By leveraging self-awareness and empathy, such leaders can navigate organizational dynamics with both compassion and clarity.

Teamwork

Teams with high emotional intelligence are more cohesive and resilient. They communicate openly, handle conflicts constructively, and support each other's growth. This dynamic results in greater productivity, innovation, and job satisfaction. Empathy and social skills are particularly vital in fostering a collaborative environment where every team member feels heard and valued.

Personal Relationships

In personal relationships, emotional intelligence helps individuals connect deeper with loved ones, resolve disagreements more amicably, and build lasting bonds based on mutual respect and understanding. Whether in friendships, romantic relationships, or family dynamics, grace enables people to engage with others in ways that nurture growth and connection.

Crisis Management

In times of crisis, emotional intelligence can make the difference between success and failure. Leaders who manage their own emotions and remain empathetic can guide their teams through challenges with steadiness and resolve. For instance, during the COVID-19 pandemic, many organizations that prioritized emotional intelligence in their leadership saw greater employee engagement and resilience compared to those that focused solely on productivity metrics.

The Transformative Power of Grace

Emotional intelligence is more than just a set of soft skills—it is the embodiment of grace in action. When cultivated and integrated with grit, emotional intelligence empowers individuals to navigate life's challenges with resilience, compassion, and integrity. Whether in leadership, teamwork, personal relationships, or crisis management, the ability to balance grit and grace leads to more meaningful connections, greater success, and a life marked by both achievement and fulfillment.

As you continue to develop emotional intelligence, remember that it is a lifelong journey. The more you invest in understanding yourself and others, the more you will enhance your capacity to lead with both strength and kindness, creating lasting impact in all areas of your life.

CHAPTER SIX

Developing Both Grit and Grace

"When people talk, listen completely. Most people never listen."
~ Ernest Hemingway

Nelson Mandela, one of the most revered figures in modern history, exemplified the qualities of mental toughness, resilience, and emotional intelligence throughout his extraordinary life. Born on July 18, 1918, in the rural village of Mvezo in South Africa's Eastern Cape, Mandela's journey from a young boy in a traditional Xhosa household to a global icon for justice and equality was marked by unwavering determination and deep emotional insight.

Mandela's early life set the stage for his later activism. He was born Rolihlahla Mandela, a name when translated in his native language means "troublemaker." This translated name would come to reflect his lifelong challenge to the status quo. Mandela's father was a local chief and counselor to the Thembu royal family, but after his father's death, Mandela was adopted by Chief Jongintaba Dalindyebo, who taught him leadership and broadened young Nelson's understanding of African politics. Educated at missionary schools and later the University of Fort Hare, one of the few higher education institutions for black South Africans, Mandela developed a keen awareness of the systemic injustices of apartheid.

Mandela's mental toughness was first put to the test as he became involved in the African National Congress (ANC) in the early 1940s. Despite growing up in a divided and oppressed society, Mandela believed in the possibility of change. This belief, combined with his ability to persevere, became the cornerstone of his activism. In 1961, he co-founded the ANC's armed wing, Umkhonto we Sizwe (Spear of the Nation), signaling a strategic shift toward armed resistance against apartheid. Although he was branded a terrorist by the apartheid regime and later by some international figures, Mandela remained resolute in his commitment to achieving equality for all South Africans.

The mental resilience Mandela exhibited was most evident during the twenty-seven years he spent in prison, mostly on Robben Island. From 1962 to 1990, Mandela endured harsh conditions, limited contact with his family, and the uncertainty of whether he would ever be freed. However, instead of breaking under these conditions, Mandela transformed this period of confinement into a time of growth and reflection. He maintained his leadership role within the ANC even behind bars, mentoring younger activists and negotiating with the apartheid government. His mental toughness was punctuated by an incredible ability to stay focused on his long-term goals despite the suffering and isolation.

During these years, Mandela's emotional intelligence was key to his survival and future leadership. He displayed remarkable self-control, empathy, and the ability to manage his emotions in ways that would later allow him to lead a deeply divided nation toward reconciliation. Understanding the need to move beyond personal grievances, Mandela emerged from prison not with a desire for revenge but with a commitment to forgiveness and unity. His famous words during his inauguration as South Africa's first black president in 1994, "I stand before you not as a prophet but as a humble servant of you, the people," reflect his deeply ingrained empathy and humility.

His resilience extended beyond his prison years as he took on the monumental task of leading South Africa through its transition from apartheid to democracy. He skillfully balanced the needs of those who had been oppressed with the fears of those who had enforced the oppression. His formation of the Truth and Reconciliation Commission, led by Archbishop

Desmond Tutu, epitomized his belief that healing could only come through confronting the past with honesty and compassion.

Moreover, Mandela's ability to understand and manage his emotions, coupled with his ability to observe, identify, and navigate the emotions of his adversaries exemplified his profound emotional intelligence. His decision to invite his former jailers to his presidential inauguration and his symbolic gesture of donning the Springbok rugby jersey—long seen as a symbol of white Afrikaner supremacy—demonstrated a sophisticated understanding of the emotional power of symbols in bridging divides. These acts helped unite a fractured nation, showing the world that emotional intelligence is not just a personal asset but a tool for societal transformation.

In his later years, Mandela continued to be a voice of moral authority, advocating for peace, human rights, and education globally. Even as he aged and withdrew from the public eye, his legacy of resilience, mental toughness, and emotional intelligence remained influential, inspiring new generations of leaders.

Mandela's grit and grace combined to create a legacy that transcends borders and generations. His resilience in the face of personal suffering and his grace in promoting peace and reconciliation turned him into a global icon of leadership and moral courage. He demonstrated that true grit is not just about enduring hardship, but about staying committed to one's values and goals, even when the path is difficult. At the same time, he showed that grace—expressed through empathy, forgiveness, and humility—is essential in creating lasting change and healing deep wounds. His life serves as an enduring reminder that the most powerful leaders are those who combine grit with grace and who can fight fiercely for justice while extending compassion to all.

Nelson Mandela's story demonstrates that personal and professional success and fulfillment do not result from isolated acts of determination or fleeting moments of emotional intelligence. Rather, they stem from consistent, daily practices that integrate grit and grace into every aspect of our routines. Developing these qualities involves more than simply knowing what they are; it requires building habits that continually strengthen resilience, perseverance, self-awareness, and empathy. This chapter explores practical strategies to integrate grit and grace into your life through intentional routines, habits, and practices.

Daily Practices for Developing Grit

Grit is not something you either have or don't have—it is a skill that can be cultivated through deliberate practice. The key is to establish daily routines that reinforce resilience and perseverance. Let's explore how you can incorporate these practices into your life.

1. Setting and Pursuing Meaningful Goals

Setting clear, achievable goals is the foundation of grit. However, the process doesn't end there. Consistently working toward those goals, even when the initial motivation fades, is what separates high achievers from others. Start by defining long-term objectives that align with your core values and break them down into smaller, actionable steps. Use a system like SMART (Specific, Measurable, Achievable, Relevant, and Time-bound) to structure these goals. For example, if your goal is to improve your health, you might break it down into daily activities like exercising for thirty minutes, preparing balanced meals, and tracking your progress weekly.

Moreover, visualization can be a powerful tool in reinforcing your commitment to these goals. By mentally rehearsing your success, you build the confidence and mental fortitude necessary to stay the course. This practice is common among top athletes and high performers, who routinely envision their success before stepping into the arena.

2. Embracing Discomfort and Challenge

Grit is about persistence, and persistence often involves stepping outside your comfort zone. Cultivating mental toughness requires regularly putting yourself in situations that challenge you. Whether it is taking on a difficult project at work, learning a new skill, or engaging in physical training, the ability to thrive under pressure is strengthened by exposure. The more you embrace discomfort, the more resilient you become when facing adversity.

Establish a routine that intentionally includes challenging tasks. This could involve setting weekly "stretch goals" that push your limits or engaging in activities that require sustained focus and effort. Over time, these practices will aid in the development of mental toughness needed to persevere through difficulties.

3. Developing Consistent Discipline

Discipline is what keeps you moving forward even when motivation is low. Building discipline starts with structuring your day around routines that promote consistency. This includes setting a regular schedule for work, exercise, and rest. The more structured your day is, the easier it becomes to develop habits that align with your goals.

One powerful strategy is the use of micro-habits—small, easily repeatable actions that require minimal effort but yield significant long-term results. For example, if you struggle with procrastination, begin with the habit of working on a task for just five minutes. Often, the momentum created in those initial minutes leads to sustained focus, making it easier to complete the task.

Another aspect of discipline is holding yourself accountable. Tracking your progress through journaling or habit-tracking apps can provide the necessary feedback to stay on course. The act of writing down your goals, reflecting on your progress, and reviewing your accomplishments regularly can reinforce your commitment and keep you aligned with your vision.

Daily Practices for Developing Grace

Grace, as we have demonstrated, is just as crucial as grit. It involves understanding and managing your emotions, as well as effectively engaging with others. To cultivate grace in your daily life, focus on enhancing the core components of emotional intelligence: self-awareness, self-regulation, motivation, empathy, and social skills.

1. Practicing Self-Reflection and Mindfulness

Mindfulness is a practice that helps you become more aware of your thoughts and emotions. By paying close attention to your internal state, you can better manage your reactions to stress and pressure. Start with a simple daily mindfulness routine, such as five minutes of deep breathing or meditation. These practices help center your thoughts, reduce stress, and enhance your ability to respond rather than react in emotionally charged situations.

Journaling is another effective tool for developing self-awareness. By regularly reflecting on your experiences, challenges, and emotional responses, you can gain insights into your behavior patterns and triggers. This reflection allows you to make intentional adjustments that improve how you manage your emotions and interactions with others.

2. Cultivating Empathy Through Active Listening

Empathy is the foundation of effective communication and strong relationships. Developing empathy starts with active listening—fully focusing on the speaker without formulating a response until he or she has finished. This type of listening requires patience, curiosity, and a genuine interest in understanding the other person's perspective.

In your daily interactions, make it a habit to listen more than you speak. Ask open-ended questions, seek clarification, and avoid interrupting. Practicing empathy helps build trust and rapport, both of which are essential in personal and professional relationships. Over time, you will find that people are more willing to collaborate and support you when they feel truly heard and understood.

3. Managing Stress and Regulating Emotions

Self-regulation is the ability to manage your emotions, especially under pressure. Developing this skill involves learning how to stay calm, focused, and composed in difficult situations. Techniques such as deep breathing, progressive muscle relaxation, and mentally reframing stressful situations can help you regain control when emotions threaten to overwhelm you.

Incorporate these techniques into your daily routine, especially during high-stress moments. For example, if you feel anxious before a big meeting, take a few minutes to practice deep breathing exercises. This simple act can lower your stress levels and improve your ability to think clearly. Over time, these practices build resilience and help you maintain emotional balance even in the most challenging circumstances.

Grit and Grace Combined

While grit and grace are often seen as separate qualities, as we have mentioned, they are deeply interconnected. Grit gives us the tenacity to pursue long-term goals, but without grace, that drive can lead to burnout, strained relationships, and poor decision-making. Conversely, grace without grit may result in compassionate but ineffective action. The key to success lies in integrating these qualities—combining resilience with emotional intelligence to achieve a balanced approach to life's challenges.

Leaders who demonstrate both grit and grace are not only able to push through troublesome situations but also inspire others to do the same by leading with empathy and understanding. This balance allows for both personal and organizational growth, fostering environments where people feel both challenged and supported.

Real-World Examples of Grit and Grace

Terry Fox – Cancer Activist and Athlete: In 1977, Fox was diagnosed with osteosarcoma and had to have his leg amputated. Instead of giving up, Fox decided to embark on the "Marathon of Hope," a cross-Canada run to raise awareness and funds for cancer research. He ran over 3,000 miles with a prosthetic leg before his cancer returned and he was forced to stop. Fox's determination to run marathon-length distances daily, despite immense physical pain, exemplified grit. His grace was evident in his calm and compassionate demeanor, never complaining about his situation but always focusing on helping others. His legacy continues to inspire millions, as his foundation has raised over $850 million for cancer research.

Maya Moore – WNBA Star and Justice Advocate: At the peak of her WNBA career, Moore stepped away from basketball in 2019 to focus on criminal justice reform, specifically to help free Jonathan Irons, a man wrongly convicted of burglary and assault. Moore spent years working on his case, and Irons was finally released in 2020 after 23 years in prison. Moore's grit was shown in her willingness to put her athletic career on hold for a cause greater than herself. Her grace was apparent in how she handled the legal fight, always speaking with humility and empathy for both Irons and those affected by the criminal justice system. Her persistence and dignity in the face of systemic injustice set a powerful example.

Roger Federer – Tennis Legend: Federer, one of the greatest tennis players of all time, faced numerous challenges throughout his career, including injuries and fierce competition from rivals like Rafael Nadal and Novak Djokovic. Yet, he consistently remained at the top of his game for nearly two decades, setting records and winning 20 Grand Slam titles. Federer's grit was evident in his long-term dedication to the sport, maintaining an elite level of performance into his late 30s. His grace shone through in the way he treated his opponents, win or lose. Known for his sportsmanship, humility, and calm under pressure, Federer always carried himself with elegance, making him a beloved figure both on and off the court.

Jonny Kim – U.S. Navy SEAL, Doctor, and NASA Astronaut: Kim's journey is remarkable. Born to South Korean immigrants, Kim overcame adversity to become a decorated U.S. Navy SEAL, completing over 100 combat missions. After his military service, he pursued a medical degree from Harvard and then became a NASA astronaut. Kim's grit is evident in his perseverance across multiple demanding careers—military, medicine, and space exploration—each requiring immense mental and physical fortitude. His grace is seen in his humility; despite his incredible accomplishments, Kim often downplays his own success and instead focuses on using his skills to serve others, whether through medicine or space research.

These individuals have not only demonstrated remarkable grit in overcoming personal and professional challenges but also embodied grace through their humility, empathy, and dignified approach to adversity. Their stories serve as powerful examples of both grit and grace in action.

The Daily Practice of Grit and Grace

Cultivating grit and grace is not about making dramatic changes overnight; it is about consistently integrating small habits and practices that align with your vision and values. By focusing on mental toughness and emotional intelligence in your daily routines, you build the foundation for long-term success and fulfillment.

Remember that both grit and grace are skills that can be developed with intentionality and effort. Whether it's setting meaningful goals, practicing mindfulness, or leading with empathy, each step you take brings you closer to embodying the qualities that define a well-rounded and resilient individual. By embedding these practices into your daily life, you not only achieve your goals but also enrich your relationships, enhance your leadership, and create a life of balance and purpose.

CHAPTER SEVEN

Leadership Implications of Grit and Grace

"The greatest leader is not necessarily the one who does the greatest things. He is the one that gets the people to do the greatest things."

~ Ronald Reagan

One of the most transformative lessons in my leadership journey came unexpectedly from an interaction early in my career, which taught me the importance of grit and grace in leadership. At the time, I was a young executive in a rapidly growing company, managing a team that included someone with far more experience than I. Despite her being almost ten years my senior, with much more corporate experience, she reported directly to me, creating somewhat of an uncomfortable dynamic. One day, she approached me outside of our regular meetings, asking if she could give me some feedback. Without much thought, I casually agreed, unaware that this conversation would fundamentally change my approach to leadership.

I remember being engrossed in my work, likely with my back to the door, when she entered my office. She patiently waited until I gave her my full attention, and then began speaking in a manner that, quite frankly, caught me off guard. She began, "I'd like to share what I've been observing, tell you how it makes me feel, and the impact it's having, and then I'd like to give you a chance to respond." Upon gaining my agreement, she calmly laid out her observations: during our weekly touch base meetings, she noticed that I often appeared to be distracted—tilting my head, my eyes glazing over, and frequently checking my watch while she spoke. This behavior, she explained, made her feel unimportant and undervalued as a team member, to the point where she had started exploring other job opportunities and even had an interview scheduled the following day.

I was stunned. She hadn't raised her voice, accused me, or made any over-generalizations about my poor leadership. She simply shared what she had observed, in extremely specific terms, and how it was affecting her. All my defenses and rebuttals vanished; there was nothing left for me to argue against. She had completely disarmed me. My immediate response was one of genuine remorse. I apologized profusely, admitting that I wasn't even aware I was doing those things. I promised her that while change might take time, she had my full permission to hold me accountable if I slipped back into those behaviors. As I reflected on that moment several days or weeks later, I realized the power of how she had approached this difficult conversation.

Reflecting on that interaction in the years that followed, I distilled the steps she took into what I now call "Feedback without Fallout." This approach has since become a cornerstone of my own leadership style whenever I need to provide tough feedback or engage in difficult conversations. Let's review.

PLAN AHEAD: The first lesson she taught me was to plan for the conversation. She clearly took the time to think through what she wanted to say, likely even practicing the conversation beforehand. This preparation allowed her to stay focused and articulate.

ASK FOR PERMISSION: She asked for and received my permission before diving into the feedback. By getting my buy-in from the outset, she created an environment where I was more receptive, knowing I had given her the green light.

OWN THE AGENDA: There was no mistaking the fact that she owned the agenda. She structured the conversation in a clear and deliberate way: laying out her observations, expressing how those observations made her feel, sharing the impact, and then inviting my response. This made the conversation logical and easy to follow, keeping emotions in check.

USE "I" MESSAGES: Another crucial aspect was her use of "I" and "me" statements. By focusing on her own experiences rather than using accusatory language, she avoided triggering defensiveness. Instead of saying, "You're always distracted," she said, "I've observed these behaviors, and they make me feel . . ." This subtle shift in language is what took the confrontation out of the equation.

SPEAK ONLY FOR YOURSELF: Additionally, she spoke only for herself. She didn't drag in what "others" might be thinking or feeling, which is a common mistake when giving feedback. By speaking solely from her perspective, she kept the discussion honest and focused.

FOCUS ON RESOLUTION: Finally, she allowed for dialogue and resolution by inviting me to respond. After delivering her message, she stopped talking and gave me the space to process and react, which made the conversation a two-way street rather than a lecture.

Leadership is the art of guiding people toward shared goals while fostering an environment that brings out the best in everyone involved. Leaders who embody grit demonstrate mental toughness, resilience, persistence, and an unwavering commitment to their goals. Do not be mistaken, it took incredible grit for my colleague to initiate this conversation with me. On the other hand, leaders who lead with grace exhibit empathy, emotional intelligence, and the ability to connect with others on a deeper level. When these qualities are combined, leaders not only achieve sustained success but also build enduring relationships and cultivate a culture of trust and collaboration. This conversation, which epitomized grit and grace, had a profound and enduring impact on my leadership from that day forward.

This experience taught me that leadership is not just about directing others but about creating environments where open communication thrives. The "Feedback without Fallout" framework is not only about minimizing conflict; it is also about ensuring that feedback leads to growth, both for the person receiving it and the one giving it. In any relationship—whether professional or personal—handling difficult conversations with courage and empathy can lead to deeper trust, greater self-awareness, and better outcomes for everyone involved.

This chapter delves into how leaders can integrate mental toughness with emotional intelligence to inspire teams, drive innovation, and navigate the complexities of modern organizational life.

Great leaders don't just rise to the occasion—they persist through it. Grit is the defining trait that separates those who merely hold positions of authority from those who drive lasting impact. It is the relentless perseverance, unwavering resilience, and ability to rebound from failure that enables leaders to navigate uncertainty and adversity. Leaders with grit don't shy away from challenges; they embrace them as steppingstones to growth. Their vision remains steadfast, guiding them through setbacks and propelling them toward success.

Grit in Leadership

Great leaders don't just rise to the occasion—they persist through it. Grit is the defining trait that separates those who merely hold positions of authority from those who drive lasting impact. It is the relentless perseverance, unwavering resilience, and ability to rebound from failure that enables leaders to navigate uncertainty and adversity. Leaders with grit don't shy away from challenges, they embrace them with courage and decisiveness, as steppingstones to growth. Their vision remains steadfast, guiding them through setbacks and propelling them toward success.

1. Perseverance and Resilience

Perseverance is the determination to continue moving forward, even when the path is difficult. Leaders who possess grit are committed to their vision and are willing to put in the hard work required to achieve it. Resilience complements perseverance by enabling leaders to bounce back from failures and setbacks. Resilient leaders don't see obstacles as roadblocks but as opportunities for growth and learning.

Real-world examples of gritty leadership include figures such as Steve Jobs, who demonstrated extraordinary resilience when he was ousted from Apple, only to return years later and lead the company to unprecedented success. Similarly, leaders such as Nelson Mandela exemplify the power of perseverance, having endured twenty-seven years in prison while maintaining his commitment to justice and equality.

2. Courage and Decisiveness

Grit also involves having the courage to make tough decisions, even in the face of opposition. Leaders with grit are willing to take calculated risks and make bold choices that align with their vision. Courageous leadership is about standing firm in your convictions while remaining adaptable enough to pivot when circumstances require it.

Courage in leadership is not just about making tough decisions; it is also about taking responsibility for those decisions. Leaders with grit own their choices, learn from their mistakes, and continuously seek to improve. This combination of courage and accountability builds credibility and trust within the organization.

3. Long-Term Vision and Persistence

Effective leaders have a clear long-term vision and remain committed to that vision over time. They understand that success is not achieved overnight but through consistent effort and perseverance. This long-term orientation helps them stay focused on what truly matters, even when short-term distractions or crises arise.

Incorporating grit into leadership means embracing the idea that progress is often slow and incremental. Leaders with grit are not easily swayed by immediate setbacks or fluctuations in external conditions. Instead, they stay the course, making steady progress toward their goals while continuously refining their strategies.

Grace in Leadership

While grit is essential for driving results, grace allows leaders to build meaningful relationships, create a positive work environment, and a thriving team culture. True leadership isn't about driving results—it is about inspiring trust, cultivating relationships, and leading with empathy and compassion. Graceful leaders balance confidence with humility, strength with understanding, and ambition with care for those they lead. They create environments where people feel valued, supported, and motivated to give their best. By mastering grace in leadership, you build not only a high-performing team, but also a legacy of trust and collaboration.

1. Self-Awareness and Emotional Regulation

Grace begins with self-awareness—the ability to recognize and understand your own emotions, strengths, weaknesses, and values. Leaders who are self-aware can better manage their reactions to stress, criticism, and uncertainty. Emotional regulation, another key component of grace, involves

maintaining composure and responding thoughtfully in high-pressure situations.

For instance, a leader who remains calm and collected during a crisis not only sets a positive example but also helps to stabilize the team. This ability to regulate emotions is critical for making sound decisions and fostering a culture of trust.

2. Empathy and Compassionate Leadership

Empathy is at the heart of grace in leadership. It is the ability to understand and share the feelings of others, and it's what enables leaders to connect with their teams on a human level. Empathetic leaders listen actively, show genuine concern for their team members, and are attuned to the needs and emotions of those they lead.

Compassionate leadership goes beyond empathy; it involves taking action to support and uplift others. Leaders who demonstrate grace through compassion create an environment where people feel valued, respected, and motivated to give their best. This approach not only boosts morale but also drives higher levels of engagement and loyalty.

3. Building Trust and Fostering Collaboration

Graceful leaders are skilled at building trust and fostering collaboration. They understand that strong relationships are the foundation of effective teamwork. By cultivating a culture of open communication, mutual respect, and shared purpose, these leaders enable their teams to work together more effectively and achieve greater results.

Collaboration is not just about working together; it is also about aligning individual strengths toward a common goal.

Leaders who embody grace encourage diverse perspectives, promote inclusivity, and ensure that everyone's voice is heard. This inclusive approach strengthens the team's ability to innovate and adapt to changing circumstances.

Integrating Grit and Grace in Leadership

The most effective leaders are those who can seamlessly integrate grit and grace into their leadership style. They are both resilient and compassionate, both results-oriented and people-centered. This balance is what enables them to navigate the complexities of modern leadership, where both high performance and positive relationships are essential for success.

1. Leading with Both Strength and Humility

Leaders who demonstrate grit set the tone for their teams by remaining committed to their vision, even in the face of adversity. At the same time, leaders who show grace are attuned to the needs of their team members, providing support, and understanding when challenges arise.

They are confident in their vision and decisive in their actions, but they are also open to feedback and willing to admit when they are wrong. Humility allows leaders to learn from others, build stronger relationships, and create a culture of continuous improvement.

2. Adapting to Change with Resilience and Empathy

In today's volatile, uncertain, complex, and ambiguous (VUCA) environment, the ability to adapt to change is critical. Leaders who combine grit and grace are resilient in the face of disruption but also empathetic in their approach to leading others through change. They understand that people respond to change differently and take the time to support their teams emotionally while guiding them toward new opportunities.

3. Inspiring and Motivating Teams Through a Shared Vision

Leadership is about inspiring others to achieve a shared vision. Leaders who integrate grit and grace inspire their teams not only through their determination and perseverance but also through their ability to connect with people on a human level. They communicate their vision with clarity and passion, and they align the team's efforts with a sense of purpose and collective responsibility.

This approach to leadership results in teams that are not only high-performing but also deeply engaged and committed to the organization's success. By leading with both grit and grace, leaders create a culture where people feel both challenged and supported—where they are encouraged to strive for excellence while knowing that their well-being is valued.

4. Encouraging Continuous Learning and Adaptability

In rapidly changing environments, adaptability is crucial. Leaders who cultivate grit and grace understand that learning and growth are ongoing processes. Encourage your team to embrace a growth mindset where setbacks are seen as learning opportunities. Provide opportunities for professional development, whether through training, mentorship, or cross-functional projects.

By integrating learning into the daily routine, you reinforce the importance of resilience and flexibility. Teams that are both gritty and graceful are better equipped to navigate uncertainty, innovate, and sustain high performance over time.

5. Creating an Accountable and Supportive Environment

A culture of grit and grace is one where high standards and mutual respect coexist. Encourage accountability by setting clear expectations and holding team members responsible for their contributions. However, also provide the necessary resources, feedback, and encouragement to help them succeed. This balance ensures that people are motivated to achieve while feeling valued and supported.

Regular team check-ins, feedback loops, and open communication channels are essential in building this culture. By fostering a supportive environment where challenges are seen as opportunities for growth rather than threats, you empower your team to develop both resilience and emotional intelligence.

Building a Culture of Excellence

Probably the best examples of Grit and Grace in Leadership come from the hundreds of existing and former clients with whom I have had the opportunity to work. Through my work with individuals, teams, and organizations around the world, I have been able to observe certain patterns within organizations that achieve sustained success over the longer-term. We have organized these patterns into a framework we call the ***"Culture of Excellence,"*** which includes the following six elements:

1. **Strong Leadership:** Organizations that generate sustained results over time first and foremost recruit, promote, and cultivate strong leadership at all levels of the organization. These leaders buy in to the organization's mission, as well as to the core values, and business strategies. They have a growth mindset and, while they are seldom perfect in balancing grit and grace, they have an earnest desire to learn, grow, and improve.

2. **Clarity and Focus:** In addition, these Strong Leaders ensure there is clarity around three major questions in the organization (1) Who are we? (the Mission, Culture, Brand Promise), (2) Where are we going? (the Vision, Long-term and Short-term goals, and Priorities, as well as the Business Strategies), and (3) How will we get there? (the Key Performance Measures, and the Individual & Collective Accountabilities). We will talk more about Clarity and Focus specifically a bit later.
3. **Engaged and Committed Teammates:** In addition to ensuring there is Organizational Clarity and Focus, high-performing leaders also ensure that teammates are recruited, selected, hired, and fired according to their buy-in and adherence to the desired culture and strategy. Engaged teammates are committed to the direction of the organization, they are individually competent, and they operate in clearly defined and accepted roles. As such, they know how their individual contributions and accountabilities contributed to the greater good of the Organization.
4. **Empowering Communication:** The word "empower" means to make someone "stronger and more confident at dealing with the circumstances they are facing." As such, empowering communication is a way of communicating that builds people up and makes them stronger and more confident. Top performing leaders, and the organizations they lead, cultivate an environment where empowering communication permeates individual and collective interaction. They move beyond mutual respect, support, and encouragement, to strengthening one another. For instance, when a leader is required to intervene into the suboptimal performance of an employee, he does not stop at calling out the performance failure; he also lays out alternate paths to success, recommends

complementary courses of action, and helps the employee develop a plan of action.

5. **100% Accountability:** This type of accountability means that my deeds match my words. When I commit to doing something, I do it, come hell or high water. At the very first indication that I sense a potential distraction on the horizon, I immediately go to the person to whom I am accountable and discuss the situation. I do not wait until the committed deadline has passed and simply hope they don't ask me about it. In this sense, 100% Accountability is highly correlated with integrity.
6. **Organizational Agility:** In the words of the great management thinker Mike Tyson, *"Everyone has a plan until they get punched in the mouth!"* This is a variation on the old saying, *"No plan survives first contact with the enemy."* Just like individuals must be resilient in facing unforeseen setbacks and challenges, high-performing teams and organizations must do the same. But beyond simple resilience in the face of adversity, agility also means to be able to think, understand, and move quickly and easily. We certainly must bounce back after being knocked down to the mat; however, agile leaders and organizations anticipate and often avoid punches by planning ahead, recognizing patterns, and moving quickly to avert disaster.

Building a culture of excellence within an organization or team requires the integration of grit and grace at both the individual and collective levels. Leaders who embody these qualities inspire their teams to do the same, setting a standard for accountability, adaptability, and sustained excellence. Teams that operate with grit stay committed to the mission and demonstrate unwavering dedication to performance. At the same time, teams that prioritize grace communicate with clarity and respect, adapt to changing circumstances, and build trust through consistent, empowering interactions. Together, these elements create an organizational culture where excellence is not just a goal, but a sustained way of operating that continually drives both individual and collective achievement.

The Path to Balanced Leadership

Winston Churchill's leadership during one of history's darkest periods is often cited as a prime example of sustained grit. Leading Britain through World War II, Churchill was relentless in his resolve; but his leadership wasn't just about grit—he balanced his determination with empathy and a deep understanding of his nation's morale. Through his speeches and actions, Churchill demonstrated both strength and compassion, helping his country endure and eventually triumph in the war.

As we conclude this chapter, the path to balanced leadership lies in the integration of grit and grace. Leaders who can master both qualities are better equipped to navigate the challenges of today's fast-paced and complex world. They can drive results while building strong, trusting relationships that sustain long-term success.

In your own leadership journey, remember that grit and grace are not opposing forces but complementary strengths. By cultivating both mental toughness and emotional intelligence, you can lead with purpose, inspire others, and create a legacy of excellence and integrity.

CHAPTER EIGHT

Building Strong Teams With Grit and Grace

"The strength of the team is each individual member. The strength of each member is the team."

~ Phil Jackson

The 1992 United States men's Olympic basketball team, famously known as the "Dream Team" is widely regarded as the greatest sports team ever assembled. Comprised of some of the biggest stars in NBA history—such as Michael Jordan, Magic Johnson, Larry Bird, and Charles Barkley—this team did not simply overwhelm their opponents with talent. They demonstrated that mental toughness and emotional intelligence are critical factors in producing sustained success at the highest levels. In a tournament where they won by an average of forty-four points per game, the Dream Team's dominance was not merely a product of superior skill; it was also a testament to the power of resilience, emotional control, and the synergy that occurs when highly driven individuals align their goals and push each other to greater heights.

For these legendary athletes, mental toughness was a prerequisite for thriving in the pressure-filled environment of Olympic competition. Michael Jordan, who was at the peak of his career, set the tone with his relentless competitiveness and focus. Known for his ability to remain composed and perform at his best even in the most intense situations, Jordan's leadership pushed the team to take every game seriously, regardless of the insurmountable gap in talent between them and their opponents. This mindset permeated the team. Even in practice sessions, famously competitive scrimmages such as the "Greatest Game Never Seen" between Magic Johnson and Jordan's squads became battlegrounds where mental toughness was continually sharpened. These internal contests laid the foundation for the collective resilience that would define their journey in Barcelona.

While their path to the gold medal appeared effortless, the Dream Team's success was rooted in the resilience of its members, many of whom were nearing the end of their careers or facing significant personal challenges. Magic Johnson's return to the court after his shocking HIV diagnosis and Larry Bird's struggle with chronic back pain highlighted their determination to compete at the highest level despite the odds. The way these players pushed through physical and emotional adversity exemplified the essence of resilience—not merely the ability to endure hardship, but the capacity to come out stronger and more committed on the other side.

But what truly set the Dream Team apart was their collective and individual emotional intelligence. Integrating a roster full of alpha personalities and transcendent talents could have easily led to tension and ego clashes, but the team's success hinged on their ability to put aside individual pride in favor of the common goal. Magic Johnson's charisma and leadership played a crucial role in fostering camaraderie and mutual respect among teammates who were often fierce rivals during the NBA season. His emotional intelligence helped create an atmosphere where every player felt valued, and where competition was fierce but never divisive. This understanding and respect for each other's strengths and roles enabled them to operate with a unity rarely seen in teams of such star power.

Coach Chuck Daly also demonstrated remarkable emotional intelligence in his management of the team. Rather than micromanaging or imposing his authority, Daly recognized that these players knew how to win and allowed them to self-regulate on the court. His decision not to call a single timeout throughout the entire Olympic tournament reflected his trust in the team's collective intelligence and his ability to guide them without stifling their instincts. Daly's light-touch approach encouraged players to take ownership of their roles and resolve challenges independently, fostering a deep sense of accountability and shared leadership.

Individually, players such as Scottie Pippen and Charles Barkley showcased emotional maturity by adapting their roles to fit the needs of the team. Pippen embraced the role of defensive anchor, sacrificing personal glory to support the team's overall success. Barkley, known for his brash personality, channeled his energy into productive competitiveness, leading the team in scoring while maintaining the balance between intensity and collaboration. Their ability to recognize what the team needed from them, combined with an elevated level of self-awareness, helped solidify the team's cohesion.

The Dream Team's run in the 1992 Olympics wasn't just a showcase of unparalleled basketball talent; it was a demonstration of how mental toughness and emotional intelligence, when aligned, can produce extraordinary results. These qualities allowed a group of superstars to transcend individual brilliance and come together as a cohesive unit, redefining what it means to be a successful team. The lessons learned from their journey continue to resonate far beyond the world of sports, offering valuable insights into the importance of resilience, emotional intelligence, and collective purpose in any high-stakes endeavor.

The Foundations of Resilient Organizations

The journey to creating resilient, high-performing teams and organizations is not merely a matter of adopting effective processes or implementing the latest technological innovations. It involves cultivating an environment where mental toughness, emotional intelligence, and collaboration thrive. Resilient organizations are those that can adapt, recover, and even thrive in the face of adversity. They achieve this by fostering cultures where both grit and grace are championed and by embedding these qualities into the DNA of the organization. In this chapter, we explore how these elements manifest within teams and organizations, shaping cultures of resilience, empathy, and sustained success.

Clarifying Organizational Grit

Grit within an organization mirrors the individual quality of perseverance, but on a collective scale. It represents the collective will and determination to achieve long-term goals despite the inevitable setbacks, challenges, and disruptions that arise. Organizational grit is about maintaining focus and commitment across all levels, ensuring that everyone, from entry-level employees to the top leadership, shares a unified vision and demonstrates resilience when facing obstacles.

Examples of organizational grit can be found in companies such as Pixar, which overcame numerous technical and creative hurdles in its pursuit of groundbreaking animation. The relentless pursuit of excellence, even in the face of repeated failure, is a hallmark of gritty organizations. This quality allows teams to maintain lofty standards, push through difficulties, and innovate in ways that might otherwise seem impossible.

Cultivating Organizational Grace

Grace within an organization manifests as a culture where empathy, compassion, and effective communication are prioritized. In such environments, leaders are attuned to the emotional needs of their teams, fostering trust and psychological safety. This aspect of organizational grace allows individuals to navigate challenges with understanding, manage conflicts effectively, and support one another through both successes and failures.

An excellent example of organizational grace is Patagonia, a company known not only for its environmental activism but also for its compassionate and collaborative culture. By integrating empathy and ethical responsibility into its values, Patagonia has built a brand that is as much about doing good as it is about doing well. This balance between organizational grit (taking bold stances and persevering through challenges) and grace (engaging in constructive dialogue and maintaining integrity) has solidified Patagonia's place as a leader in both business and social impact.

Strategies for Embedding Grit and Grace Into Organizational Culture

To build resilient teams and organizations, it is essential to intentionally cultivate grit and grace across all levels. Here are several strategies that leaders can adopt to embed these qualities into their organizational culture:

1. **Establishing Clear, Shared Goals:** One of the most effective ways to instill grit in an organization is to create a shared vision that everyone is committed to. It has been said that "Without involvement, there will be no commitment." Engaging team members in the formulation of a team's vision is the best way to ensure that vision is shared. Additionally, when teams have a clear understanding of the long-term direction and see how their contributions fit into the bigger picture, they are more likely to stay focused and persevere during challenging times. This shared vision creates alignment and motivates employees to push through difficulties as they work toward a common goal.
2. **Fostering a Growth Mindset:** Encouraging a growth mindset is key to developing both grit and grace. A growth mindset is the belief that abilities and intelligence can be developed through hard work,

learning, and persistence. Organizations that promote this mindset create an environment where challenges are viewed as opportunities for growth rather than threats. This perspective not only builds resilience but also enhances emotional intelligence by encouraging employees to learn from feedback and approach problems with curiosity and flexibility.

3. **Building Psychological Safety and Trust:** Grace flourishes in environments where trust is high, and people feel psychologically safe to express themselves without fear of ridicule or retribution. Leaders play a crucial role in creating such environments by modeling vulnerability, encouraging open communication, and actively listening to team members. Psychological safety allows employees to share ideas, voice concerns, push back against "group think," and take risks without the fear of negative repercussions. This environment is critical for fostering innovation and collaboration, as people are more likely to contribute their best ideas when they feel supported.
4. **Integrating Resilience and Empathy Into Leadership Development:** Leadership development programs should include training in both grit and grace. Resilience training helps leaders develop the mental toughness needed to navigate crises and maintain focus on long-term goals, while emotional intelligence training enhances their ability to lead with empathy, build strong relationships, and manage team dynamics effectively. By equipping leaders with these dual skill sets, organizations can ensure that their leadership bench is strong and prepared to guide teams through both turbulent and prosperous times.
5. **Promoting Collaboration and Shared Accountability:** A culture of grit and grace is one where collaboration is prioritized, and success is seen as a collective effort rather than the result of individual heroics. In such cultures,

teams work together toward common goals, holding each other accountable while providing mutual support. Leaders should remove silos, encourage cross-functional collaboration, create opportunities for team members to learn from one another, and recognize collective achievements as much as individual contributions.

Real-World Examples of Grit and Grace in Action

To illustrate how grit and grace manifest in real-world organizations, let's examine a few case studies that highlight these qualities in action.

The 2010 Chilean Miners Rescue

The rescue of the thirty-three Chilean miners trapped underground for sixty-nine days stands as a powerful example of both grit and grace in organizational efforts. The international rescue team, composed of engineers, medical professionals, and rescuers, faced extreme challenges in executing the operation. The grit displayed in their unwavering determination to succeed, despite the high stakes and technical difficulties, was complemented by grace—evident in the team's ability to collaborate effectively, manage emotions under pressure, and prioritize the well-being of the trapped miners. The successful rescue was not only a triumph of technology but also a testament to the power of perseverance and compassionate leadership.

Pixar's Culture of Creativity and Resilience

Known for its groundbreaking films, Pixar's creative process is marked by a willingness to embrace failure and learn from it. The studio's leaders foster a culture in which taking risks, experimenting with novel ideas, and supporting one another are valued as much as achieving commercial success. By combining relentless pursuit of excellence with a deeply empathetic approach to team dynamics, Pixar has been able to produce a series of films that resonate with audiences worldwide while maintaining a culture of innovation and collaboration.

Microsoft's Cultural Transformation Under Satya Nadella

Since taking over as CEO in 2014, Satya Nadella has led a remarkable cultural transformation at Microsoft. By emphasizing emotional intelligence, fostering a growth mindset, and pursuing ambitious goals, Nadella shifted the company's focus from internal competition to collaboration and customer-centric innovation. This cultural shift has been credited with revitalizing Microsoft, leading to significant growth and innovation. Nadella's balanced focus grit and grace at the organizational level has been key to Microsoft's resurgence as a leader in the tech industry.

The Long-Term Impact of Grit and Grace in Organizations

Leaders who recognize the importance of balancing results with relationships can build teams that are both high-performing and deeply connected. By embedding these principles into every aspect of the organization—from leadership development and team collaboration to daily interactions—companies can create cultures that not only withstand adversity but also thrive in it. The path forward for resilient, compassionate, and successful organizations is clear: embrace both grit and grace as essential qualities for sustained growth and impact. Organizations that successfully integrate grit and grace into their cultures are better equipped to navigate the complexities of today's business environment.

CHAPTER NINE

Navigating Crisis and Adversity With Grit and Grace

"The ultimate measure of a man is not where he stands in moments of comfort and convenience, but where he stands at times of challenge and controversy."

~ Martin Luther King Jr.

When Alan Mulally took the helm as CEO of Ford Motor Company in 2006, the iconic automaker was on the verge of collapse. With plummeting sales, declining market share, and billions in losses, Ford's future looked bleak. In the face of such adversity, Mulally's leadership became a masterclass in navigating through a crisis with a blend of mental toughness and emotional intelligence. His journey exemplifies how grit and grace can be used to guide organizations through turbulent times, transforming near-certain failure into remarkable success.

Upon taking over, Mulally inherited a company burdened by inefficiencies, internal divisions, and a culture of fear and denial. The automotive industry was rapidly changing, but Ford had failed to innovate at the pace of its competitors. Mulally recognized that turning Ford around required more than just cutting costs and restructuring—it demanded a cultural shift. This is where his mental toughness and emotional intelligence came into play.

One of Mulally's first actions was to implement a unified vision called "One Ford," which aimed to bring every part of the company together under a single mission. This vision wasn't just a slogan; it became a rally cry for everyone at Ford. Mulally's mental toughness was evident in his unwavering commitment to this vision, even when faced with resistance from those who were skeptical of his outsider status or who clung to the old ways of doing things. He knew that meaningful change would be met with pushback, yet he maintained his resolve and stayed focused on the long-term goal.

A key component of Mulally's leadership was his insistence on transparency and accountability. He introduced a weekly business plan review meeting, where executives were expected to openly share the status of their projects—both successes and failures. Initially, there was fear in the room; Ford's culture had long been one where admitting failure was seen as career suicide. However, Mulally used his emotional intelligence to create psychological safety where leaders could discuss their challenges without fear of retribution. He would often respond to reports of setbacks with support rather than criticism, encouraging his team to focus on finding solutions rather than dwelling on problems. This approach fostered trust, collaboration, and a willingness to take risks—all crucial elements in Ford's turnaround.

One of the most telling examples of Mulally's emotional intelligence was his reaction when Mark Fields, a senior executive, openly admitted in one of the meetings that his team was struggling with a critical product launch. In the old Ford, this kind of admission might have led to harsh consequences. Instead, Mulally clapped and thanked Fields for his honesty, signaling to the entire company that vulnerability and transparency were now valued. This moment was a turning point; it showed that Mulally wasn't just focused on the numbers—he cared about the people behind those numbers. His ability to connect with employees on a human level was key to transforming Ford's culture from one of fear to one of shared purpose.

Mulally's mental toughness was further tested when he made the controversial decision to mortgage all of Ford's assets—including its iconic blue logo—to secure a $23.5 billion loan. This bold move gave Ford the liquidity it needed to invest in new products and weather the economic downturn without resorting to a government bailout, which many of its competitors, such as General Motors and Chrysler, relied on. Mulally's decision, which required both courage and conviction, saved the company and allowed Ford to emerge from the crisis stronger than ever. Throughout his tenure, Mulally demonstrated that true leadership in crisis isn't just about making tough decisions; it is about doing so with empathy, integrity, and a deep understanding of human dynamics. He didn't just lead with strategy; he led with heart. By balancing mental toughness with emotional intelligence, Mulally was able to turn Ford around not just financially, but culturally. His story illustrates that resilience in the face of adversity requires more than just grit—it requires grace, humility, and the ability to connect with others on an emotional level.

Mulally's leadership at Ford serves as a powerful example for leaders navigating their own crises. It is a reminder that even in the most challenging circumstances, the combination of mental toughness and emotional intelligence can turn obstacles into opportunities and create lasting success.

In life, few things test our resolve like crises and adversity. Whether it's a personal setback, a family emergency, or an organizational crisis, these challenges force us to dig deep, confront our vulnerabilities, and find strength in places we did not know existed. The journey through adversity is a powerful crucible where the elements of grit and grace come to life. In this chapter, we will explore how these qualities manifest in times of crisis, drawing from real-world examples and strategies that emphasize perseverance, resilience, empathy, and emotional intelligence.

The Nature of Crisis: A Test of Character

Crises are inevitable in both personal and professional spheres. They come in various forms—financial turmoil, health scares, relational breakdowns, or global events like pandemics and geopolitical conflict. What sets apart those who not only survive but thrive in these situations is not merely the strategies they employ but the character they embody. Grit and grace are at the core of such character.

Grit and Grace in Times of Adversity

As we have demonstrated previously in multiple examples, grit and grace are not independent qualities; they are deeply interconnected, especially during crises. When life throws unexpected challenges our way, it is not enough to simply push through with determination—we must also be attuned to the emotional needs of ourselves and others. This balance between perseverance and empathy creates the conditions for not just overcoming adversity but emerging stronger and more connected.

One of the key aspects of navigating crises with grit and grace is resilience, which is the ability to bounce back from setbacks and maintain emotional stability. Emotional regulation is critical in this process. During high-stress situations, it is easy for fear, frustration, and anger to take over, but those who possess emotional intelligence can manage these feelings and remain level-headed. This emotional regulation not only allows them to make better decisions but also creates a calming influence on those around them.

Grace manifests through empathy, particularly in how we listen and respond to others. In a crisis, people often need more than solutions—they need to feel heard, understood, and supported. Leaders who practice active listening and genuinely consider the emotions and perspectives of others foster trust and cooperation, which are essential in navigating complex challenges. This form of grace is what allows teams, families, and communities to pull together during tough times.

Real-World Examples of Grit and Grace in Crises

Let's look at several real-world stories that exemplify the power of grit and grace in navigating some of the toughest challenges life can present.

The Response to Hurricane Katrina

In 2005, Hurricane Katrina devastated the Gulf Coast, leaving behind a trail of destruction and displacing hundreds of thousands of people. The crisis highlighted both the challenges and triumphs of human resilience. On one hand, the disaster exposed failures in emergency preparedness and government response, but it also revealed the strength and determination of those who rose to help their communities rebuild.

Stories emerged of everyday citizens who, despite losing everything, came together to rescue neighbors, provide shelter, and rebuild their communities. Nonprofit organizations and volunteers from across the country demonstrated both grit in their sustained efforts and grace in their compassionate response. This blend of qualities was critical in helping many find hope amid the chaos.

Pixar's Journey Through Near Bankruptcy

Pixar, now a powerhouse in the animation industry, nearly collapsed before it produced its first major hit, *Toy Story.* The early years of the company were marked by financial instability and creative struggles. The founders, including Steve Jobs, John Lasseter, and Ed Catmull, had to demonstrate extraordinary grit to keep pushing forward when investors and even employees were losing faith in their vision.

Yet, what set Pixar apart was not just their perseverance but also the grace with which they handled internal conflicts and setbacks. The leadership at Pixar emphasized open communication, creativity, and mutual respect, which created a culture that could weather crises and emerge stronger. The combination of grit and grace turned Pixar's near failure into a story of remarkable success and innovation.

Johnson & Johnson and the Tylenol Crisis

In 1982, Johnson & Johnson faced one of the most significant crises in corporate history when several people died after taking cyanide-laced Tylenol capsules in the Chicago area. The crisis sent shockwaves through the nation, leading to widespread fear, and plunging the company into turmoil. Tylenol was a leading pain reliever at the time, representing a sizable portion of Johnson & Johnson's revenue. The company's immediate response would not only determine its future but also set a new standard for crisis management. The grit shown by Johnson & Johnson's leadership during this crisis was exemplified by their swift decision-making. Despite the potential financial fallout, the company issued a nationwide recall of over 31 million bottles of Tylenol, costing them over $100 million. This bold move demonstrated an unwavering commitment to consumer safety over short-term profits, even when there was no guarantee the brand would recover.

What truly defined their response, however, was the grace with which they handled the situation. Johnson & Johnson's leadership, under CEO James Burke, openly communicated with the public, the media, and government agencies throughout the crisis. They provided clear, transparent updates and took full responsibility, even though the tampering occurred outside of their production facilities. This transparency and accountability helped rebuild trust with consumers and stakeholders.

In addition to the recall, Johnson & Johnson introduced tamper-resistant packaging, which became an industry standard and drastically improved consumer safety nationwide. Their actions were driven by a genuine concern for public well-being, balanced by strategic decisions to protect and restore the brand. This combination of grit in tackling the crisis head-on and grace in prioritizing integrity and transparency helped Johnson & Johnson not only recover but also strengthen their reputation in the long run. Today, the Tylenol crisis is frequently cited as a gold standard in effective crisis management.

Strategies for Cultivating Grit and Grace in Crisis

As we have previously established, the impact of grit and grace spans innumerable scenarios, situations, and circumstances. Even the most extreme crises can be overcome with the delicate balance of grit and grace. Navigating such crises with grit and grace is a skill that can be cultivated. Here are practical strategies for individuals and leaders to develop these qualities:

1. **Develop a Growth Mindset:** Adopting a growth mindset—believing that challenges are opportunities for learning and growth—is fundamental to building resilience. Developing a growth mindset requires us to reframe resistance, roadblocks, and/or setbacks as learning opportunities. Those who see adversity as a temporary setback rather than a permanent roadblock are more likely to persevere and find creative solutions for moving forward.
2. **Practice Mindfulness and Emotional Regulation:** Mindfulness practices, such as meditation and journaling, help individuals stay grounded during stressful times. Learning to regulate your emotions ensures that you can respond thoughtfully rather than react impulsively when faced with pressure.
3. **Build Strong Relationships and Support Networks:** Grace is often reflected in how we connect with others during challenging times. By building strong, trusting relationships before a crisis occurs, you create a network of support that can be leaned on when adversity strikes. This is true not just in personal relationships but in organizational cultures as well.
4. **Embrace Compassionate Leadership:** For leaders, navigating crises with grace involves showing empathy, being transparent in communication, and remaining calm under pressure. Compassionate leadership builds

trust and encourages others to rise to the occasion, knowing that their efforts are both valued and supported.

5. **Focus on Long-Term Goals While Adapting Short-Term Strategies:** Crises often require leaders to shift strategies in the short term while keeping an eye on long-term objectives. Balancing immediate needs with the overarching vision is a hallmark of leading with both grit and grace.

The Transformative Power of Grit and Grace in Adversity

Crises have a way of revealing the true character of individuals and organizations. Those who successfully navigate these challenges do so by embodying both grit and grace—by combining unwavering perseverance with deep empathy and emotional intelligence. Whether it is personal hardships, professional challenges, or global crises, the ability to remain resilient while also extending compassion to others is what transforms adversity into a powerful catalyst for growth.

As we move forward, it is essential to recognize that while crises are unavoidable, our response to them is within our control. By cultivating grit and grace in our lives, we can not only survive the storms but also find new strength, purpose, and connection on the other side.

CHAPTER TEN

Measuring and Tracking Progress in Grit and Grace

"What gets measured gets improved."

~ Peter Drucker

Cultivating grit and grace is an ongoing journey that requires intentional practice, self-reflection, and consistent effort. Whether you are striving to build mental toughness, enhance emotional intelligence, or both, it is essential to measure and track your progress. Why? Because without a clear sense of where you are and how far you have come, it is difficult to know where to focus your efforts next. This chapter simplifies the process of assessing and improving grit and grace, offering practical strategies and real-world examples to guide your journey.

Why Measuring Grit and Grace Matters

At first glance, grit and grace might seem like abstract qualities, challenging to quantify. But they can be measured, evaluated, and improved over time—just like any other skill. By assessing your growth in grit and grace, you gain insights into your strengths and identify areas where you can improve.

Psychologist Angela Duckworth, who popularized the concept of grit, found that it often predicts achievement better than talent alone. Tracking your grit helps you understand how well you stay focused on your goals, especially when faced with obstacles or distractions. By regularly assessing your grit, you can identify patterns and adjust your strategies to maintain motivation and persistence.

Measuring grace allows you to see how well you manage your emotions and interact with those around you. This is essential for building trust, resolving conflicts, and leading others effectively.

Practical Tools for Measuring Grit and Grace

There are several tools and methods available to measure your growth in grit and grace. Whether you prefer self-assessment questionnaires or want to observe real-life behavior, the right tools can provide you with valuable feedback.

Self-assessment is one of the simplest ways to measure your grit and grace. Self-assessments offer a starting point for understanding your current state, but they are most useful when combined with other methods. These tools allow you to reflect on your own behavior and mindset, giving you a clear picture of your strengths and areas for growth.

- **The Grit Scale:** Developed by Angela Duckworth, the Grit Scale measures two key aspects of grit: consistency of interests and perseverance of effort. This tool asks you to reflect on statements such as, *"I am diligent and never give up easily,"* and *"I have a hard time staying focused on projects that take more than a few months to complete."* Your responses provide a snapshot of your current level of grit.

- **Mental Toughness Inventory (MTI):** The MTI was developed by researchers John Mahoney, Daniel Gucciardi, Marc Mallet, John Ntoumanis, and Cliff Mallett to create a more streamlined and efficient measure of mental toughness, as existing measures were often complex and multifaceted. Their goal was to design a single-factor tool that captures the essence of mental toughness without overcomplicating the assessment process. The MTI is a self-report inventory that evaluates how individuals handle stress, pressure, and challenges. It provides insights into one's ability to stay focused and resilient in demanding situations.

- **MTQ48 and MTQPlus:** The MTQ48 was developed by Peter Clough, Keith Earle, and Doug Strycharczyk. It measures mental toughness across four components: control, commitment, challenge, and confidence. The MTQPlus is an updated version of the MTQ48, offering a more comprehensive look at mental toughness while still measuring the same four core components. It was also developed by Clough and colleagues. These tools are widely used in both professional and educational settings to assess and develop mental toughness.

- **The Trait Emotional Intelligence Questionnaire (TEIQue):** The TEIQue was developed by K. V. Petrides to assess trait emotional intelligence, which refers to a constellation of emotional self-perceptions located at the lower levels of personality hierarchies. With the TEIQue, emotional intelligence is assessed across key areas such as self-awareness, emotion management, and empathy. It provides insights into how well you understand and regulate your emotions, as well as how effectively you navigate social interactions.

- **The Emotional Quotient Inventory (EQ-i 2.0):** The EQ-i 2.0, developed by Dr. Reuven Bar-On, is a self-report assessment that measures emotional intelligence across five key areas: self-perception, self-expression, interpersonal skills, decision-making, and stress management. This tool helps individuals gain insight into their emotional strengths and weaknesses, providing a roadmap for improving leadership, communication, and personal effectiveness.

- **The Self-Report Emotional Intelligence Test (SREIT):** The SREIT, created by Dr. Nicola Schutte and colleagues, is based on the ability model of emotional intelligence developed by Salovey and Mayer. This assessment evaluates an individual's perceived emotional intelligence through 33 self-assessment items, focusing on emotional perception, regulation, and utilization. It helps individuals reflect on their emotional competencies and identify areas for growth in personal and professional settings.

Behavioral observations provide a relatively objective view of how you demonstrate grit and grace in real-life situations. Instead of relying solely on how you perceive yourself, this approach assesses your actual behavior in challenging or emotionally charged moments.

- **The Emotional and Social Competency Inventory (ESCI 360):** The ESCI 360, developed by Dr. Daniel Goleman and Richard Boyatzis, is a multi-rater assessment that evaluates emotional intelligence based on feedback from peers, managers, subordinates, and other colleagues. It measures key emotional competencies such as self-awareness, self-management, social awareness, and relationship management. By incorporating external perspectives, the ESCI 360 provides a well-rounded view of a leader's emotional effectiveness and interpersonal impact.

- **The Mayer-Salovey-Caruso Emotional Intelligence Test (MSCEIT):** The MSCEIT is a performance-based test that measures emotional intelligence (EI) based on the ability model of EI proposed by Mayer and Salovey. This tool evaluates emotional intelligence through a series of tasks that test how you perceive, understand, and manage emotions. By assessing how you respond to specific scenarios, the MSCEIT provides a more accurate picture of your emotional intelligence in action.

- **The EQ 360 (Multi-Rater Version of EQ-i 2.0):** The EQ 360, an extension of the EQ-i 2.0 developed by Dr. Reuven Bar-On, is a multi-rater assessment that incorporates feedback from colleagues, supervisors, and direct reports to provide a comprehensive evaluation of emotional intelligence. By comparing self-perceptions with external observations, the EQ 360 offers valuable insights into how an individual's emotional intelligence is perceived in real-world interactions, making it a powerful tool for leadership development and team dynamics improvement.

- **The Grit-S Scale (Observer-Rated Version):** The Grit-S Scale, originally developed by Dr. Angela Duckworth, is a widely used self-assessment tool that has been adapted into an observer-rated format. This version allows colleagues, supervisors, or mentors to assess an individual's perseverance and passion for long-term goals. It measures two key dimensions of grit: consistency of interest and perseverance of effort. By incorporating external perspectives, this assessment provides a more objective evaluation of how an individual demonstrates grit in professional or academic environments.

- **The Grit-360 Assessment:** The Grit-360 is a multi-rater assessment designed to evaluate grit through feedback from peers, managers, and subordinates. It measures an individual's commitment to long-term goals, resilience in the face of setbacks, and sustained effort over time. This tool highlights differences between self-perception and external observations, offering valuable insights for leadership development, team dynamics, and personal growth. By capturing how grit is perceived by others, the

Grit-360 helps identify strengths and areas for improvement in persistence and resilience.

- **The Grit Behavioral Interview Framework:** The Grit Behavioral Interview Framework is a structured observation-based assessment used in hiring, talent development, and leadership evaluations. Developed from Dr. Angela Duckworth's research, this method assesses grit through scenario-based questions that prompt individuals to describe past experiences related to perseverance, adaptability, and long-term goal commitment. Responses are evaluated using a standardized rubric, providing a behavioral measure of grit. This framework is commonly used in executive coaching and performance assessments to identify individuals who demonstrate sustained effort and resilience in real-world situations.

Establishing feedback loops by continuous tracking progress in grit and grace is an ongoing process. Regular feedback, whether from self-reflection, peer reviews, or coaching, is essential for reinforcing growth. Effective feedback loops include:

- **Journaling and Self-Reflection:** Journaling allows you to document your emotional responses, track your behavior patterns, and assess how you are evolving over time. Reflecting on your experiences can help you identify triggers, strengths, and areas where you need improvement.

- **Goal Setting and Progress Reviews:** SMART goals (Specific, Measurable, Achievable, Relevant, Time-bound), as previously discussed, are a reliable framework for tracking progress. By setting specific milestones and regularly reviewing your achievements, you can see where you are making strides and where adjustments are needed. Regular check-ins, whether weekly or monthly, ensure that you stay on track and maintain momentum.

Measuring Grit and Grace in Different Settings

To bring these concepts to life, let's explore a few examples of how grit and grace have been measured and developed in different settings.

Grit in Education

In schools, educators have increasingly used the Grit Scale to help students stay focused on their academic goals. For instance, in a high school in California, students took the Grit Scale assessment at the beginning of the year. Based on their scores, they were grouped for targeted support, such as study skills workshops and peer mentoring programs. Over the course of the year, students with initially low grit scores showed marked improvement in both perseverance and academic performance after participating in these programs.

Grace in Corporate Leadership

In a multinational company's leadership development program, emotional intelligence assessments were used to enhance leaders' ability to connect with their teams. Executives were given the MSCEIT assessment, followed by one-on-one coaching sessions that focused on areas like stress management, active listening, and conflict resolution. Over six months, leaders who engaged in the program showed significant improvements in team engagement scores and employee satisfaction.

Combining Grit and Grace in High-Stress Professions

In high-stakes fields such as emergency response and the military, balancing grit and grace is critical. During disaster response simulations, teams are assessed not only on their ability to stay focused and make decisions under pressure but also on how they manage the emotional well-being of their colleagues. Teams that score high in both grit (for completing the mission) and grace (for maintaining team cohesion) are often the most successful in real-world crises.

The U.S. military cultivates mental toughness and resilience through a comprehensive approach that includes rigorous training, psychological conditioning, and the fostering of an unbreakable team spirit. In the Army, resilience and mental toughness are systematically developed through Basic Combat Training (BCT), which pushes soldiers to confront physical exhaustion, mental stress, and fear. Through challenging drills such as the Confidence Course, forced ruck marches, and sleep deprivation, soldiers are trained to embrace discomfort and remain focused under pressure. Resilience is also cultivated through the Army's Master Resilience Training (MRT) program, which incorporates elements of positive psychology to equip soldiers with the mental tools needed to manage stress, overcome adversity, and maintain a mission-first mindset.

The Marines, known for their intense focus on shared hardship, place a strong emphasis on building a warrior ethos through events such as the Crucible, a fifty-four-hour test of endurance that is designed to break down and rebuild recruits with a mindset of perseverance and unity. Similarly, Navy SEAL training—considered among the toughest in the world—pushes candidates through grueling exercises in BUD/S (Basic Underwater Demolition/SEAL) training, where they are taught to maintain focus, self-regulation, and adaptability under extreme conditions.

The U.S. Navy SEALs employ a technique known as "mental rehearsal", which is similar to visualization but incorporates more senses, making the rehearsal as real as possible. SEALs also practice the 40 percent rule, a belief that when your mind is telling you you're done, you are only forty percent done, and you have more to give.

Across all branches, a common principle is the importance

of teamwork and trust. Soldiers, Marines, and SEALs learn that resilience is not just about individual toughness but also about relying on the team and maintaining the resolve to accomplish the mission no matter the circumstances. By consistently exposing service members to high-stress environments and conditioning them to manage their responses, the military forges individuals who are both mentally tough and resilient in the face of adversity.

The Journey to Grit and Grace

The path to mastering grit and grace is one of continuous growth. By measuring your progress, reflecting on feedback, and applying strategies for improvement, you can steadily develop these qualities in your life. Remember, the goal isn't perfection but consistent progress. By committing to this journey, you will not only achieve your goals but also enrich your relationships, lead with greater impact, and find deeper fulfillment.

As you continue to integrate grit and grace into your life, take time to celebrate small victories, learn from setbacks, and remain open to the growth that comes from embracing both perseverance and empathy. The balance you strike between these qualities will not only shape your personal and professional success but also leave a lasting impact on those around you.

CHAPTER ELEVEN

The Power of Vision

"Leadership is the capacity to translate vision into reality."
~ Warren Bennis

In the early 1980s, Seattle was home to a small coffee bean and coffee brewing equipment retailer. At the time, it was far from the global giant we know today, but it was beloved by its local patrons—coffee enthusiasts who were drawn to its high-quality beans and appliances. Howard Schultz first encountered Starbucks in 1981, when he was the director of Sales for a company that sold housewares. Starbucks was one of his accounts, and Schultz was intrigued by the passion of the company's founders and their commitment to quality.

But during a visit to Milan, Italy, Schultz had a revelation. There, coffee bars were not just places to get a quick caffeine fix; they were social hubs. They were the heartbeats of neighborhoods, where people met, conversed, and took a break from the pace of daily life. Schultz envisioned bringing this concept to America, transforming Starbucks from a simple bean seller into a "third place" between home and work.

When Schultz shared this vision with the Starbucks founders, they weren't sold. They believed that selling drinks would dilute the company's original mission. But Schultz's vision was so compelling, he could not let it go. He left Starbucks and founded his own coffee chain, Il Giornale, to test his idea. His company quickly grew, and when Starbucks' founders decided to sell their business, Schultz acquired it. With Starbucks now under his control, Schultz was free to fully realize his vision.

Clarity, Focus, and Execution: The Trinity of Achievement

Achieving your goals requires more than just setting them. It requires clarity, focus, and impeccable execution. These three elements work together to ensure that you remain on track and avoid distractions.

CLARITY: Clarity is the foundation of effective planning and goal setting. It involves knowing exactly what you want and why you want it. Ideally, clarity begins with having a crystal-clear understanding of the destination at which you desire to arrive yourself, or with your team or organization. This over-arching clarity is called your Vision. Clear goals are the tools used to bring a high-quality vision to fruition. They are not vague aspirations; they are well-defined targets that leave no room for ambiguity. The clearer your goals are, the more likely you are to achieve them, and the more likely you are to bring your vision into reality. Clarity also helps you communicate your vision and goals to others, making it easier to enlist support and resources along the way.

FOCUS: Focus is the discipline to stay committed to your goals despite distractions, setbacks, or competing priorities. In today's fast-paced world, distractions are everywhere. Social media, emails, and the demands of daily life can easily pull you off course. To achieve your goals, you need to maintain a laser-like focus on what truly matters. This means saying "no" to anything that does not align with your vision and goals. Successful people are masters of focus—they prioritize their goals above all else and consistently direct their energy toward achieving them.

EXECUTION: Execution is where the rubber meets the road. It is not enough to have a sharp vision and well-defined goals; you must take consistent action to bring those goals to life. Execution involves planning, organizing, and taking deliberate steps toward your goals every day. It is about turning ideas into reality through disciplined effort and persistence. Remember, it's not the goals themselves that lead to success, but the consistent actions taken toward achieving them.

The Power of Vision-Casting

One of Schultz's strengths as a leader was his ability to cast a clear, compelling vision that rallied others to his cause. He didn't just see what Starbucks could become; he communicated that vision with passion and clarity, inspiring employees, investors, and customers alike. Schultz knew that vision alone wasn't enough—he needed everyone in the organization to see what he saw.

From the beginning, Schultz emphasized that Starbucks was about more than coffee; it was about creating an experience. He frequently articulated this vision in meetings, town halls, and training sessions. He told stories of his time in Italy, painting vivid pictures of bustling coffee bars where relationships were formed, ideas were shared, and communities thrived. He used those stories to build a bridge between his vision and the day-to-day actions required to achieve it. Starbucks employees were no longer just baristas; they were ambassadors of a culture centered around connection, community, and quality.

Discovering the Impact of Vision

You may wonder why a chapter on vision and goal setting has been inserted into a book on Mental Toughness and Emotional Intelligence. It is because I have witnessed it repeatedly throughout my career—successful people have a future orientation. They know where they are going. They may not know exactly how they're going to get there, but they do have a clear vision of their intended destination, and they set an aligned set of goals, actions, and tasks or habits to get there. Underlying this vision is a three-step framework involving Clarity, Focus, and Execution

I first learned the magnitude of this powerful trifecta by accident. I often tell people that I crammed a four-year degree into almost six years, meaning it took me longer than most, because I worked full-time throughout my entire college journey. I worked as an emergency medical technician (EMT) and a paramedic for a hospital-based ambulance service. I decided to complete my degree in Respiratory Therapy for one simple reason—I wanted to be a member of the flight team aboard Angel One, the helicopter based at Arkansas Children's Hospital.

The first day of the professional portion of the respiratory therapy program, I waltzed into the department director's office at Arkansas Children's Hospital and declared, "*When I graduate, I'm going to come here and join your helicopter team. So, if you'd like to hire me now, you can train me during the next year, so I'll be ready when I graduate.*"

Pretty bold, huh? Needless to say, I did not get the job that day; however, a few months later, after observing me during a clinical rotation for my Respiratory Therapy program, that same department director hired me. The day after I graduated, I was a fully trained member of the Angel One Flight Team. I spent the next nine years living my dream. Fate had another surprise in store for me. I met and got to know another member of that team—a cute little flight nurse—who came to be my wife, Lori.

Successful, mentally resilient people are very deliberate about where they are going. They have clarity about their intended destination. They develop a relentless focus on that destination, and they know how to impeccably execute against the plan to get there.

While grit and grace provide the necessary resilience and empathy to tackle challenges, it is vision that illuminates the path ahead and goal-setting that transforms aspirations into actionable steps. Without a clear destination, even the most determined effort can become misdirected and fruitless. This chapter explores the integral roles that vision and goal setting play in achieving success and how they provide the clarity, focus, and direction needed to fully leverage grit and grace.

Setting Goals That Drive Organizational Success

Vision without concrete goals is a daydream, but Schultz paired his grand vision with clear, measurable objectives. He set audacious yet achievable targets, such as opening thousands of stores in new markets, ensuring consistency across locations, and maintaining a premium brand. Schultz knew that if Starbucks was to scale globally, it needed a structure that could support rapid growth without sacrificing quality. This required rigorous operational goals focused on training, supply chain management, and customer experience.

To sustain Starbucks' growth and ensure alignment with the company's vision, Schultz embedded goal setting into the organization's culture. He established processes where goals were set, measured, and refined at every level of the company—from corporate offices to individual stores. This disciplined approach allowed Starbucks to scale while maintaining the essence of what made the brand special. Every goal set was tied back to the overarching vision, reinforcing a shared purpose across the organization.

Sustained Success Through Adaptation and Resilience

As Starbucks grew, it faced inevitable challenges: market saturation, competition, and economic downturns. However, Schultz's vision remained a constant guiding force. During the 2008 financial crisis, Starbucks experienced declining sales and store closures. Many questioned whether the company could maintain its trajectory. Schultz returned as CEO and immediately went back to the foundational vision, even as he adapted to new market realities. He closed underperforming stores, re-trained thousands of baristas to refocus on quality, and doubled down on the customer experience. These moves reinforced the original vision while setting new goals to align with a rapidly changing business landscape.

The Impact of Vision-casting

Under Schultz's leadership, Starbucks grew from a small regional company to a global brand with thousands of stores in over seventy countries. What made this transformation possible was not just operational excellence or clever marketing; it was the combination of a compelling vision, and the relentless pursuit of goals aligned with that vision. Schultz didn't just build a company; he built a culture where vision and goals were intertwined in a way that drove sustained success.

Howard Schultz's journey with Starbucks is a testament to the power of vision-casting and goal setting. His ability to see beyond the obvious, to articulate a compelling future, and then to set goals that brought that future into reality is what made Starbucks a global icon. Leaders who master these principles can transform not only their businesses but also the lives of the people they serve.

The Significance of Vision: Seeing the Destination

Vision is the foundation upon which all successful endeavors are built. It is the vivid picture of the future that motivates and drives us forward. Vision defines not only where we want to go, but also who we want to become along the way. It encompasses both our highest aspirations and our core beliefs for the future. Vision sets the tone for our journey, shaping our decisions, actions, and even the people with whom we choose to surround ourselves.

One of the most famous examples of the power of vision is President John F. Kennedy's bold declaration in 1961, that the United States would *"land a man on the moon before the end of the decade."* At the time, this vision seemed impossible, yet it galvanized a nation and led to one of humanity's greatest achievements. This is the power of vision: it aligns resources, focuses efforts, and brings together disparate forces to accomplish something extraordinary.

In my own career, vision has been a constant guide. Early on, I discovered that those who succeeded consistently were those who had a clear picture of their destination. They weren't necessarily the most talented or the hardest working, but they knew exactly where they were going and why. This clarity of vision allowed them to remain focused even when faced with obstacles and distractions.

The vision you craft for your life or career should be bold yet grounded in your values and strengths. It should excite you, challenge you, and push you beyond your current capabilities. However, vision alone is not enough—it needs to be coupled with intentional goal setting.

Crafting a Compelling Vision

To create a compelling vision, you must begin by understanding your deepest desires, values, and aspirations. This requires introspection and the willingness to dream big. Allow yourself to imagine the kind of life you want to live, the impact you want to make, and the person you want to become. Visualization is a powerful tool in this process. Top athletes, entrepreneurs, and leaders often use visualization techniques to picture their desired outcomes, which helps them align their actions with their goals.

When crafting your vision, ask yourself the following questions:

- *What do I genuinely want to achieve in my life and career?*
- *What legacy do I want to leave behind?*
- *What values and principles are most important to me?*
- *How do I want to be remembered by others?*

If casting a vision for a team or organization, adapt the questions to something like the following:

- *What problem are we solving, and why does it matter?*
- *What is the ultimate impact we want to make?*
- *What outcomes do we want to be known or recognized for?*
- *What unique value do we bring to our customers or stakeholders?*
- *What does success look like in 3–5 years?*

By answering these questions, you begin to form a picture of your ideal future. Once your vision is clear, the next step is to break it down into specific, actionable goals.

Turning Vision into Reality with Goal setting

While vision provides the "where" and the "why," goal setting gives you the "how." Goals are the milestones along the path to your vision. They transform your aspirations into actionable steps, ensuring that you make consistent progress toward your destination. Without clearly defined goals, even the most inspiring vision can remain a distant dream, unattainable and abstract.

To be most effective, goals must be well crafted (SMART)—Specific, Measurable, Achievable, Relevant, and Time-bound. This framework helps ensure that your goals are clear and actionable, making it easier to track your progress and stay motivated. For example, if your vision is to become a successful entrepreneur, a SMART goal might be: *Launch a profitable online business that generates $100,000 in revenue within 12 months.* This goal meets all the criteria of the SMART framework.

It is important to recognize that goal setting is not a one-time event. It is an ongoing process that requires regular review and adjustment. As you grow and as your circumstances change, your goals may need to evolve. Flexibility is key to maintaining alignment between your goals and your vision.

Overcoming Obstacles with Grit and Grace

Even with a precise vision and well-defined goals, the road to success is rarely smooth. Challenges, setbacks, and unexpected detours are inevitable. This is where grit and grace come into play. Grit provides the resilience and determination needed to stay the course, while grace allows you to navigate challenges with empathy, flexibility, and perspective.

When pursuing ambitious goals, it is common to encounter periods of doubt, frustration, and even failure. It is during these times that grit becomes essential. Grit is the ability to persevere through adversity, to keep pushing forward even when the path seems uncertain, or progress is slow. Grit turns setbacks into opportunities for growth and learning, rather than reasons to quit.

At the same time, grace helps you manage the emotional and interpersonal challenges that arise along the way. Grace allows you to maintain perspective, stay grounded in your values, and build positive relationships even in the face of difficulties. It is the grace to forgive yourself for mistakes, to ask for help when needed, and to show compassion toward others who are part of your journey.

Together, grit and grace create a balanced approach to goal setting. Grit keeps you moving forward, while grace ensures that you do so with integrity, kindness, and respect for yourself and others.

Accountability and Progress Monitoring

To achieve personal or professional goals, accountability and progress tracking are essential. Establishing mechanisms that keep you on course significantly increases your chances of success. Accountability can come from both external and internal sources. External accountability often involves mentors, coaches, or peers who provide guidance, support, and encouragement. Internal accountability, on the other hand, comes from systems you create yourself—such as progress tracking, self-reflection, and regular check-ins.

Tracking your progress is about more than simply measuring outcomes. It involves setting clear metrics that reflect your movement toward achieving your goals. While traditional Key Performance Indicators (KPIs) are common in business, you can develop personalized metrics that align with your specific goals. These indicators help you determine whether you are on the right track and highlight where adjustments might be necessary. For instance, if you are focused on improving your health, metrics like the number of workouts per week or energy levels throughout the day might be more relevant than standard KPIs. Similarly, in business, you might track sales growth, client retention, or new leads generated.

Reflection is another critical aspect of accountability. Regularly setting aside time—whether weekly or monthly—to review your progress creates space for both celebration and recalibration. During these reviews, you not only assess how close you are to achieving your goals but also learn from the setbacks you encounter along the way. This practice fosters resilience and keeps your efforts aligned with your evolving priorities.

At its core, accountability ensures that you remain responsible for your actions, while progress tracking offers clear insights into your journey. Together, these mechanisms help you maintain focus, adjust strategies as needed, and build momentum toward long-term success.

Integrating Vision and Goal Setting Into Daily Life

The final step in making your vision and goals a reality is to integrate them into your daily routines and habits. Consistency is key. Small, daily actions build momentum over time and lead to meaningful results. Whether it is setting aside time each morning to plan your day, reviewing your goals before bed, or tracking your progress in a journal, the habits you cultivate determine your level of success.

To ensure that your vision and goals remain a priority, create a visual representation of them. This could be a vision board, a mind map, or a list of affirmations. Place it somewhere you see every day to keep your goals top of mind and reinforce your commitment.

By embedding your vision and goals into your daily life, you create a powerful system that propels you toward success, no matter the challenges that arise. As you continue to align your actions with your vision and goals, you will find that each step forward brings you closer to the life you have envisioned.

The Path Forward

Vision and goal setting are not just tools for achieving success—they are the guiding principles that shape your journey. By developing an unclouded vision and setting well-defined goals, you create a roadmap that directs your energy and effort toward what truly matters. Combined with grit and grace, these principles form a powerful framework for turning dreams into reality.

As you continue to develop and refine your vision, remember that it is a dynamic process. Your vision may evolve over time as you grow, learn, and gain new experiences. Stay committed to your goals, remain flexible in your approach, and trust that the combination of clarity, focus, and execution will lead you to success.

CHAPTER TWELVE

Powerful Examples of Grit and Grace

"Men trust their eyes rather than their ears; the road by precept is long and tedious, by example short and effectual."

~ Seneca

While I am by no means perfect, I consider myself to be pretty knowledgeable and fairly well skilled when it comes to balancing results and relationships, mental toughness, and emotional intelligence—grit and grace. But I would be less than honorable if I did not tell you that, a few years ago, I committed one of the single greatest failures in my leadership career.

A situation occurred in which one of my friends and trusted colleagues made a commitment to me, in return for a professional favor, and then I felt he violated that commitment. Upon seeing that perceived violation, I responded in a manner that violated every core belief about leadership and personal integrity that I have developed over years of experience in dealing with people. I failed to regulate my emotions. I failed to give "feedback without fallout," and I absolutely abandoned any grace I may have cultivated over the years. As a result of my abhorrent behavior, I completely ceded all high ground in a situation where I believed I was right. I gave up any rights I had in the situation because I responded so negatively and, quite frankly, behaved so badly.

Once I had calmed down, a day or two later, I became completely embarrassed by my response, my language, and my behavior. Almost everything I said and did was unprofessional and uncalled for. Even my wife was embarrassed by the way I behaved, saying to me, *"Jeff, in our thirty-plus years of marriage, I've never seen you respond to any situation like this."* I still get humiliated when I think of how I treated my friend and colleague . . . even as I write this, I feel myself blushing with embarrassment.

Once I came to terms with my complete and utter failure, there was nothing left to do but to call my friend and apologize. I explained that there was no excuse for my behavior. While I did not excuse what I believed was a violation of our agreement, I did admit that I had completely sacrificed any right I may have had to claim the high ground. I did only what I could do . . . I apologized and I asked for his forgiveness.

I will never forget how my friend responded to my request. Without hesitation he said, *"Jeff, I will always choose to forgive someone who authentically asks for it."* Such a graceful and emotionally intelligent response. While the details of the situation are irrelevant, the lessons are profound. Of course, no one is perfect. We are all human and, as such, we all have the tremendous ability to completely screw things up. But one person's empathy, emotional control, and willingness to forgive can mend a relationship that has been injured by another person's misbehavior.

Wrapping Up

It is essential to understand that the pursuit of grit and grace is not a specific destination but a continuous journey. Life is unpredictable, and it is unrealistic to expect that we will exhibit peak levels of both grit and grace every single day. Instead, the journey is one of persistence, growth, and balance—sometimes we succeed in maintaining that balance, and sometimes we fall short. What matters most is the willingness to embrace the process, learn from our experiences, and commit to ongoing growth.

As we have explored grit and grace together, we have examined how these two qualities shape lives, drive success, and inspire change. We have examined the transformative power of two qualities that, when combined, become powerful drivers of success, fulfillment, and resilience. Grit is the force that keeps us moving forward when the path is steep, ensuring we remain focused on our goals despite setbacks and adversity. Grace, on the other hand, balances that determination with empathy, compassion, and the emotional intelligence needed to connect meaningfully with others. Repeatedly, we see that true excellence is not achieved through sheer determination alone, nor is it solely the result of emotional intelligence—rather, it is the intentional balance of both. Together, these qualities create a dynamic synergy that empowers us, not only to achieve, but to do so with integrity, kindness, and purpose.

To reinforce these principles and illustrate their impact across diverse backgrounds, industries, and life experiences, we present a collection of compelling examples below. Everyone profiled here has demonstrated extraordinary grit in overcoming obstacles, setbacks, and adversity, while also cultivating the grace necessary to connect with others, lead with wisdom, and navigate challenges with emotional intelligence. Their stories serve as powerful reminders that resilience and empathy are not opposing forces, but complementary strengths that, when combined, can produce lasting success and meaningful contributions to the world.

As for you, do you know how you will process and apply the information we have discussed? My recommendation is that you commit to integrating grit and grace into your life, knowing that the rewards are not just in what you will achieve but in the legacy you will create. Lead with determination and empathy. Show resilience in the face of adversity while remaining compassionate toward yourself and others. And most importantly, embrace the journey with an open heart and a willingness to grow. The path ahead may be challenging, but it is one that leads to a life of significance, fulfillment, and lasting impact.

And, when you fall off the horse—which you will—get up, dust yourself off, climb back in the saddle, and keep riding. Trust me, you will be glad you did!

Jelly Roll

Born as Jason DeFord, Jelly Roll is a country-rap artist who emerged from an environment of hardship, criminal entanglements, and personal battles, transforming his life to achieve stardom. His story, filled with adversity and redemption, stands as a testament to the power of Grit and Grace, two qualities that he has embodied throughout his journey.

Jelly Roll grew up in a rough neighborhood of Nashville where crime and violence were pervasive. His family faced financial struggles, and from an early age, he found himself involved in street life, which led him into a cycle of incarceration. In his late teens and early twenties, Jelly Roll was arrested multiple times, primarily for drug-related offenses, and eventually spent considerable time in prison. His criminal background put him at odds with society's expectations and deeply affected his self-perception, reinforcing a sense of hopelessness. However, this was also a pivotal period, marking the beginning of his journey toward self-discovery and transformation.

Demonstrating Grit: Resilience in the Face of Adversity

Grit is exemplified in Jelly Roll's unwavering commitment to overcome his past and create a better future. Despite his criminal record and numerous setbacks, Jelly Roll's time in prison ignited a newfound determination. While incarcerated, he began writing songs and reflecting on his life, using music as an outlet to channel his struggles and aspirations. This practice built his resilience as he poured his pain and past into lyrics, transforming what could have been a permanent detour into a powerful catalyst for change. Upon his release, he faced the daunting task of reentering society, battling stigmas, and overcoming the long odds stacked against him. Yet, he remained determined to succeed in music—a goal that demanded relentless dedication in the face of rejection, personal demons, and self-doubt.

His early days in the music industry were challenging. Jelly Roll lacked formal industry connections and faced barriers due to his background, but his resilience shone through. He independently produced music, performing in small venues, and uploading his tracks online, gaining a grassroots following. His commitment to his craft—despite financial hardships, instability, and a lack of resources—demonstrates the core of Grit: the ability to endure hardship while steadily working toward a long-term vision.

Demonstrating Grace: Emotional Intelligence and Personal Growth

In addition to his grit, Jelly Roll's rise is marked by his emotional intelligence—his Grace. Throughout his journey, Jelly Roll developed a keen understanding of his emotions, a critical skill that allowed him to move beyond anger and bitterness to embrace gratitude, forgiveness, and self-compassion. By acknowledging his flaws and reflecting on his past, he cultivated self-awareness that transformed his personal narrative.

Jelly Roll's lyrics resonate deeply with his fans because they are authentic and raw. He openly addresses themes of regret, redemption, and resilience, creating an emotional connection with his audience by sharing his vulnerability. This openness has become his defining characteristic, demonstrating Grace in how he relates to others. Rather than hiding his past, he embraces it, encouraging fans to find strength in their own struggles. His humility, self-awareness, and willingness to grow are qualities that resonate, making him relatable and inspirational. Jelly Roll's empathy, both for his fans and himself, has fostered a unique bond that goes beyond typical artist-fan relationships. He understands his audience because he shares their pain, and this connection is what sets him apart.

From Prison to Stardom: The Power of Grit and Grace

Today, Jelly Roll is a celebrated music artist, known for his unique fusion of country, rap, and rock. His path to fame was neither easy nor conventional, but it is his grit and grace that made it possible. By persevering against the odds and cultivating emotional intelligence, Jelly Roll has redefined his life, transforming from a man haunted by his past into a symbol of resilience and redemption. His story illustrates that success is not defined solely by talent but by the determination to overcome adversity and the humility to connect meaningfully with others.

Vice President J.D. Vance

J.D. Vance, Vice President-elect of the United States at the time of this writing, rose from a life of hardship and adversity in Appalachia to become a best-selling author, U.S. Senator, and now, a national leader. His journey reflects remarkable resilience (Grit) and an empathetic understanding of America's struggles (Grace), shaped by his own experiences in poverty and his desire to bridge the divides in society.

Early Life and Challenges

Born in Middletown, Ohio, and raised in a struggling Rust Belt community, Vance faced a challenging childhood marked by poverty, family instability, and exposure to addiction. His mother's battles with substance abuse and his family's financial hardships were compounded by the sense of hopelessness that pervaded his community. Despite these difficult circumstances, Vance found support from his grandmother, whom he affectionately called

"Mamaw." She instilled in him the values of hard work, resilience, and the belief that he could rise above his environment.

While his early years were marked by struggle, these experiences would later serve as the foundation for his empathy and understanding of the issues facing working-class Americans. Vance's determination to break free from his circumstances led him to join the Marine Corps, a decision that would profoundly shape his future.

Demonstrating Grit in Adversity

Vance's grit is evident in his commitment to overcoming the odds stacked against him. After serving in the Marine Corps, where he gained discipline and purpose, he pursued higher education, attending Ohio State University and later Yale Law School. His transition from a poor Appalachian community to one of the most prestigious law schools in the country was no easy feat. At Yale, Vance often felt out of place among his privileged peers, but he remained determined to succeed, drawing strength from his background and the values instilled in him by his family.

Following law school, Vance went on to write *Hillbilly Elegy*, a memoir that recounts his life story and the struggles of working-class Americans. The book became a best-seller and a cultural touchstone, bringing national attention to the issues of poverty, addiction, and economic decline in the heartland. Vance's grit shines through in his ability to turn his personal hardships into a platform for advocacy, using his story to shed light on the challenges faced by millions of Americans.

Demonstrating Grace in Bridging Division

Alongside his grit, Vance's grace is evident in his empathy for the struggles of others. In *Hillbilly Elegy*, he writes with compassion and understanding about the people in his community, refusing to reduce their experiences to stereotypes or simplistic narratives. His reflections show a deep awareness of the systemic issues that contribute to poverty and addiction, as well as an appreciation for the resilience of those who persevere despite these challenges.

As he transitioned to a career in politics, Vance brought this empathy to his role as a U.S. Senator, advocating for policies that address the needs of working-class Americans and striving to bridge the gap between urban and rural communities. His commitment to understanding the concerns of his constituents and his efforts to find common ground reflect his grace. Vance has often emphasized the importance of unity, calling for compassion and understanding to heal the divisions in American society. His life experiences give him a unique perspective, allowing him to connect with people from all walks of life.

From Appalachia to the Vice Presidency: The Power of Grit and Grace

Today, J.D. Vance's journey from a troubled childhood in Ohio to the office of Vice President exemplifies the power of grit and grace. His resilience in overcoming adversity and achieving success, paired with his empathy and commitment to understanding the struggles of others, have made him a powerful advocate for unity and change. Vance's story is a testament to the belief that true leadership requires both strength and compassion—the grit to rise above personal hardships and the grace to use one's experiences to uplift others. As Vice President, he stands as a symbol of hope for those who seek a better future and a reminder that resilience and empathy can create a lasting impact.

Viola Davis

Viola Davis, acclaimed actress and the first African American woman to achieve the "Triple Crown of Acting" (winning an Oscar, Emmy, and Tony), has journeyed from poverty and adversity to one of the most respected figures in Hollywood. Her story is one of unwavering perseverance (Grit) and a commitment to authenticity and empathy (Grace).

Viola grew up in abject poverty in Rhode Island, facing hunger, bullying, and discrimination. These early experiences could have easily defined her, but instead, they fueled her desire to succeed. Viola found solace in acting, where she could escape her circumstances and express herself, eventually earning a scholarship to the prestigious Juilliard School.

Demonstrating Grit: Rising Through Adversity in Hollywood

Breaking into Hollywood as a Black woman was no easy feat. Viola encountered typecasting and racial bias throughout her career. Despite these setbacks, she remained resolute in her dedication to her craft, consistently taking roles that demanded emotional depth and authenticity. Her grit is evident in her persistence, as she continued to defy the limitations placed upon her, choosing roles that challenged stereotypes and showcased the full complexity of human experience.

Her breakthrough came with her performance in *Doubt* (2008), followed by *The Help* (2011), which earned her an Academy Award nomination and cemented her as a powerful figure in Hollywood. Viola's journey is marked by her ability to persevere, defy expectations, and reshape the narrative of Black women in film.

Demonstrating Grace: Empathy and Authenticity in Advocacy

Viola's grace is evident in her commitment to authenticity and her empathetic engagement with her audience. She openly shares her personal story, advocating for women of color and children living in poverty, and encouraging others to find strength in vulnerability. Her advocacy extends beyond her acting career as she continues to speak out on issues of race, equality, and representation in Hollywood. Viola's grace shines through in her dedication to uplifting others and using her platform to inspire change.

From Poverty to Stardom: The Power of Grit and Grace

Viola Davis's journey from hardship to acclaim exemplifies grit and grace. Her perseverance and resilience, combined with her empathy and authenticity, have not only redefined what it means to be a leading lady in Hollywood but also provided hope and inspiration to countless individuals worldwide.

Trevor Noah

Trevor Noah, comedian and former host of *The Daily Show*, rose from a challenging childhood in apartheid-era South Africa to become a global icon of comedy and social commentary. His journey reflects immense resilience (Grit) and a unique ability to bridge cultural divides with empathy and humor (Grace).

Born to a Black South African mother and a white Swiss father during apartheid, Trevor's very existence was illegal. He faced constant challenges, from navigating the racial tensions of South Africa to growing up in poverty. Despite these obstacles, his mother instilled in him a love for learning and a sense of resilience, which became his guiding forces.

Demonstrating Grit: Rising in Comedy and Overcoming Adversity

Trevor's grit is evident in his journey from small comedy clubs in South Africa to the global stage. Facing language barriers and cultural differences, he used his background as a source of humor, connecting with audiences by sharing the often-absurd realities of his upbringing. His persistence paid off, eventually landing him the role of *The Daily Show* host, a position that brought both challenges and intense public scrutiny. Through it all, Trevor's tenacity and dedication allowed him to rise above adversity, using his wit and humor to address complex social and political issues.

Demonstrating Grace: Connecting Through Empathy and Humor

Trevor's grace is embodied in his empathetic approach to storytelling. He uses humor to connect people from diverse backgrounds, breaking down complex issues with compassion and understanding. His memoir, *Born a Crime*, showcases his ability to blend humor with vulnerability, inviting readers to reflect on serious issues while seeing life through his eyes.

Trevor's grace extends to his interviews and interactions, as he consistently engages with respect and open-mindedness, allowing his platform to serve as a voice for those often unheard.

From South Africa to Global Fame: The Power of Grit and Grace

Trevor Noah's journey from apartheid South Africa to international stardom exemplifies the power of grit and grace. His resilience and adaptability, coupled with his empathetic and humorous outlook, have transformed him into a bridge between cultures, proving that perseverance and compassion can change lives.

Dwayne "The Rock" Johnson

Dwayne "The Rock" Johnson, known globally for his roles in professional wrestling and Hollywood, has journeyed from hardship to one of the most successful entertainers in the world. His story is a testament to grit and grace, highlighting a relentless drive toward success balanced with humility and kindness.

Growing up in a financially struggling household, Johnson faced many hardships. His father was a professional wrestler, often traveling to make ends meet, and Dwayne himself faced eviction and homelessness at an early age. A natural athlete, he found solace in football, eventually earning a scholarship to the University of Miami. But a terrible injury ended his football career, plunging him into a period of uncertainty and self-doubt. Determined not to let his circumstances define him, he made the choice to pursue professional wrestling—a decision that would change his life.

Demonstrating Grit: Overcoming Challenges and Rising to Fame

Johnson's grit is evident in his journey to wrestling stardom. He trained tirelessly, developing his skills and crafting his now-iconic wrestling persona, "The Rock." His perseverance paid off, leading him to become one of the most popular wrestlers of all time. Later, he transitioned to acting, where he faced another uphill battle, overcoming the stereotype that wrestlers couldn't be serious actors. Through relentless hard work and a dedication to excellence, Johnson steadily built a film career, becoming one of Hollywood's highest-paid actors.

Demonstrating Grace: Emotional Intelligence and Giving Back

Johnson is known for his grace and kindness. He often connects with fans, shares his vulnerabilities on social media, and speaks openly about his struggles with depression and mental health. His charisma and empathy allow him to engage meaningfully with his audience, making him one of the most beloved public figures. Moreover, he gives back generously, both financially and through mentorship, proving his commitment to lifting others as he rises.

From the Wrestling Ring to Hollywood: The Power of Grit and Grace

Dwayne Johnson's journey from adversity to global fame exemplifies the power of grit and grace. His resilience, hard work, and empathy have earned him a place in both the hearts of his fans and the Hollywood elite. Johnson's story is a reminder that true strength lies not only in overcoming obstacles but in staying grounded, connecting with others, and giving back.

Tim Cook

Tim Cook, CEO of Apple Inc., stepped into the shoes of one of the most visionary figures in tech history, Steve Jobs, and has since led Apple to unprecedented success while embodying the qualities of grit and grace. His journey reflects not only his resilience in maintaining Apple's legacy but also his empathy and forward-thinking approach to leadership.

Tim Cook grew up in a small town in Alabama where he developed a strong work ethic and a commitment to integrity. After graduating from Auburn University and later earning an MBA from Duke, Cook worked for companies like IBM and Compaq, excelling in operations and supply chain management. His meticulous approach and dedication eventually led him to Apple, where he was hired by Steve Jobs in 1998. Cook's contributions proved instrumental in transforming Apple's supply chain and operational efficiency, a role that would prepare him for the challenges ahead.

Demonstrating Grit: Leading Apple Through Transition

Cook's grit became clear when he took over as CEO following Steve Jobs' death in 2011. With Apple's future uncertain and under intense public scrutiny, Cook faced the daunting task of preserving Jobs' legacy while evolving Apple's vision. Cook led Apple through several major transitions, overseeing the development of groundbreaking products like the Apple Watch, AirPods, and services such as Apple Music and Apple TV+. He also expanded Apple's focus on environmental sustainability and privacy, navigating challenges with resilience and an unwavering commitment to Apple's core values.

Under his leadership, Apple became the first publicly traded U.S. company to reach a market value of over $1 trillion. Cook's perseverance through challenges—from managing global supply chain complexities to handling public scrutiny over innovation—shows his resilience and ability to sustain Apple's legacy while steering it into new directions.

Demonstrating Grace: Empathy, Inclusion, and Corporate Responsibility

Tim Cook is known for his grace, reflected in his empathetic and inclusive approach to leadership. As one of the first openly gay Fortune 500 CEOs, Cook has used his platform to advocate for LGBTQ+ rights and diversity in the workplace, creating a culture at Apple that values authenticity and inclusivity. He emphasizes corporate responsibility, championing environmental sustainability, education, and human rights initiatives.

Cook's empathetic approach extends to his vision for Apple's impact on society, prioritizing user privacy, clean energy, and accessibility. By openly addressing these values and connecting with employees and consumers alike, he has fostered a company culture that values ethics alongside innovation.

From Alabama to Apple's Helm: The Power of Grit and Grace

Tim Cook's journey from a small-town upbringing to the helm of one of the world's most influential companies exemplifies grit and grace. His resilience in guiding Apple through a critical transition, combined with his empathy and dedication to corporate responsibility, reflects a powerful blend of strength and compassion. Cook's story is a testament to the idea that true leadership requires not only strategic acumen but also a commitment to inclusivity, integrity, and societal impact.

Emma Gonzalez

Emma Gonzalez, an activist and survivor of the 2018 Marjory Stoneman Douglas High School shooting in Parkland, Florida, has emerged as a leading voice in the fight for gun control. Her story of resilience (Grit) and empathetic activism (Grace) exemplifies how one young person's courage and compassion can spark change on a national level.

Raised in Florida, Emma was a high school senior when a mass shooting claimed the lives of 17 of her classmates and teachers. The tragedy left her deeply affected, but rather than succumbing to despair, she and her classmates mobilized to advocate for safer gun laws. Driven by a sense of duty to honor those who were lost, Emma took on the public spotlight with maturity beyond her years, becoming one of the founders of the March for Our Lives movement.

Demonstrating Grit: Speaking Out Despite Criticism

Emma's grit shines in her bold stance on gun control reform and her unwavering commitment to making schools safer. She stood before millions, challenging lawmakers, and demanding action, even when faced with criticism and backlash. Known for her powerful speeches, including her viral address at the *March for Our Lives* rally in Washington, D.C., Emma captivated audiences with her directness and fearlessness. Despite being attacked by opponents and facing intense media scrutiny, she stayed resolute in her mission, traveling the country to speak at rallies, engage with lawmakers, and push for meaningful change.

Demonstrating Grace: Empathy and Advocacy for All

Emma's grace is clear in her empathy and inclusive approach to advocacy. She has consistently emphasized the importance of uniting people from all backgrounds in the fight for common-sense gun reform, listening to other survivors, and working alongside community members and activists to create a more compassionate and aware society. She has openly shared her vulnerabilities, speaking about the emotional toll the shooting took on her and her friends. Her willingness to show empathy, even in her own pain, has allowed her to connect with others affected by similar tragedies, fostering a sense of unity and shared purpose.

From Parkland Survivor to National Advocate: The Power of Grit and Grace

Emma Gonzalez's journey from high school student to national activist exemplifies the power of grit and grace. Her resilience and courage in the face of tragedy, paired with her empathetic approach to advocacy, have made her a symbol of hope and determination for a generation calling for change. Emma's story reminds us that even in the darkest of times, courage and compassion can create a path forward, empowering others to join in the pursuit of a safer future.

Naomi Osaka

Naomi Osaka, a world-renowned tennis champion, has appeared as a voice for mental health and social awareness while excelling at the highest levels of her sport. Her journey reflects not only exceptional perseverance (Grit) in the face of adversity but also a dedication to empathy and personal well-being (Grace) that inspires others.

Born in Japan to a Haitian father and Japanese mother, Naomi moved to the United States as a young child and grew up navigating multiple cultures. Her parents recognized her athletic potential early on and dedicated themselves to helping her develop her talent in tennis. As a teenager, Naomi, known for her powerful serve and quiet determination, trained rigorously and eventually broke into the international tennis circuit. By 2018, she captured her first Grand Slam title at the U.S. Open, an event that showcased her extraordinary skill and sportsmanship.

Demonstrating Grit: Overcoming Pressures and Staying at the Top

Naomi's grit is clear in her relentless pursuit of excellence despite the immense pressures of professional tennis. Rising to the top of her sport brought heightened media attention, scrutiny, and the weight of high expectations. Osaka faced challenges unique to her youthful age, including intense competition, racial and cultural barriers, and the constant pressure to perform. She went on to win four Grand Slam titles, an achievement that solidified her status as one of the top athletes in the world. Her resilience and dedication to her sport have allowed her to overcome many obstacles, consistently competing at the highest level and inspiring young athletes worldwide.

Demonstrating Grace: Prioritizing Mental Health and Advocating for Change

Naomi's grace is most evident in her willingness to advocate for mental health and social issues, setting a powerful example by prioritizing her well-being and standing up for her beliefs. In 2021, she made headlines when she chose to withdraw from the French Open to prioritize her mental health, sparking an international conversation about the pressures on athletes. Despite facing criticism, Naomi's decision highlighted her empathy for others facing similar struggles and her commitment to advocating for mental health awareness.

Beyond mental health, Naomi has used her platform to raise awareness on social issues, from racial injustice to anti-Asian hate crimes. She consistently shows compassion and thoughtfulness, connecting with her audience and encouraging conversations that extend beyond tennis.

From Tennis Prodigy to Global Advocate: The Power of Grit and Grace

Naomi Osaka's journey from a young tennis prodigy to a global icon of sport and social consciousness exemplifies the power of grit and grace. Her resilience on the court, combined with her empathy and advocacy off it, has made her a role model for athletes and fans alike. Naomi's story is a testament to the importance of perseverance and self-care, reminding us that true strength includes the courage to stand up for oneself and others.

Ruth Bader Ginsburg

Ruth Bader Ginsburg, a trailblazing Supreme Court Justice, reshaped American law with her relentless fight for gender equality. Her journey from a young woman facing discrimination to one of the most influential legal minds in history highlights her extraordinary persistence in the face of opposition (Grit) and compassion and ability to build consensus (Grace).

Early Life and Challenges

Born in 1933 in Brooklyn, New York, Ruth Bader Ginsburg grew up in a working-class Jewish family. Her mother, who instilled in her a love of education, died the day before her high school graduation. Despite this personal tragedy, she excelled academically, earning a place at Cornell University and later attending Harvard Law School—one of only a handful of women in her class.

While at Harvard, she balanced rigorous coursework with

caring for her husband, Marty, who was battling cancer. She also faced institutional sexism, with law professors and peers doubting her abilities simply because she was a woman. Instead of giving in to discouragement, she transferred to Columbia Law School, where she graduated first in her class.

Demonstrating Grit:
Fighting for Equality Against All Odds

Despite her stellar academic record, Ginsburg faced gender discrimination in her early career. Law firms refused to hire her because she was a woman, and she struggled to find opportunities in the legal profession. Undeterred, she turned to academia and became a professor at Rutgers Law School, where she began laying the groundwork for her life's work: advocating for gender equality.

As a lawyer, she argued six landmark gender discrimination cases before the Supreme Court, winning five. Her relentless pursuit of justice and her ability to strategically frame gender equality as a human rights issue—not just a women's issue—helped dismantle decades of legal discrimination.

Demonstrating Grace:
Balancing Passion with Diplomacy

Ginsburg's grace was demonstrated in her ability to form relationships across ideological lines. Despite being a champion for liberal causes, she maintained a deep friendship with conservative Justice Antonin Scalia. She understood that persuasion, not just opposition, was key to changing minds.

Her grace also extended to how she mentored young lawyers, particularly women, ensuring that the next generation had better opportunities than she did. She carried herself with quiet dignity, choosing strategic battles rather than reactive confrontation, making her an effective advocate for change.

From Law Professor to Supreme Court Icon: The Power of Grit and Grace

Ruth Bader Ginsburg's journey exemplifies resilience and emotional intelligence. She fought tirelessly for gender equality despite institutional resistance, yet she did so with civility, strategic patience, and unwavering dedication. Her legacy continues to inspire those who seek justice through perseverance and wisdom.

Noah Galloway

Noah Galloway, a former United States Army soldier, overcame life-altering injuries to become a motivational speaker and athlete, embodying Grit through his resilience and Grace through his dedication to inspiring others.

Early Life and Challenges

Born in 1981 in Birmingham, Alabama, Galloway enlisted in the Army in 2001, inspired by a family history of military service. During his second deployment to Iraq in 2005, he was severely injured by an improvised explosive device (IED), resulting in the loss of his left arm above the elbow and left leg above the knee. This traumatic event led to a period of depression and physical rehabilitation.

Demonstrating Grit: Overcoming Physical and Emotional Adversity

Despite his injuries, Galloway refused to be defined by his circumstances. He embraced fitness and took part in various competitions, including Tough Mudder and CrossFit events. His determination led him to become a personal trainer and motivational speaker, sharing his journey to inspire others facing challenges.

Demonstrating Grace: Inspiring and Supporting Others

Galloway's Grace is seen in his efforts to motivate and support others. He founded the No Excuses Charitable Fund, helping organizations like Operation Enduring Warrior and local programs such as the YMCA in Alabaster, Alabama. His participation in "Dancing with the Stars" demonstrated his ability to inspire audiences nationwide, promoting a message of resilience and positivity.

From Battlefield to Inspiration: The Power of Grit and Grace

Noah Galloway's journey from a life-threatening injury to becoming a symbol of perseverance and empathy illustrates the profound impact of balancing Grit and Grace. His story continues to inspire individuals to overcome adversity and support their communities.

Robert F. Kennedy

Robert F. Kennedy (RFK), younger brother of President John F. Kennedy (JFK), transformed from a political insider to a passionate advocate for social justice. His life was defined by his relentless fight for civil rights, justice, and the underprivileged (Grit), and his ability to unite people through empathy and moral conviction (Grace).

Early Life and Challenges

Born into the wealthy Kennedy family, RFK's early life seemed privileged, yet he lived in the shadow of his older brother, John. He served in the Navy, attended Harvard and the University of Virginia Law School, and eventually became a key figure in JFK's administration. However, his early political career was marked by ruthless ambition, earning him the nickname "ruthless Bobby." After JFK's assassination in 1963, RFK underwent a profound transformation. His grief deepened his empathy, shifting his focus from power politics to a moral crusade for justice.

Demonstrating Grit: Championing the Voiceless

As a U.S. Senator, RFK became a relentless advocate for civil rights, fighting against racial injustice and poverty. He supported the Civil Rights Act, worked to combat poverty in Appalachia, and challenged America's involvement in Vietnam. His ability to push through political resistance and remain committed to unpopular causes proved his resilience.

Demonstrating Grace: Uniting a Divided Nation

RFK's grace was seen in his emotional intelligence and ability to bring people together. His most famous moment came on April 4, 1968, when he delivered an impromptu speech in Indianapolis upon learning of Martin Luther King Jr.'s assassination. Instead of inflaming tensions, RFK spoke of unity, quoting Aeschylus and urging Americans to reject violence.

From Power to Moral Leadership: The Power of Grit and Grace

RFK's journey from political strategist to compassionate leader is a testament to the power of transformation. His resilience in fighting for justice, paired with his deep empathy, made him one of the most inspiring figures of his era.

Ella Baker

Ella Baker was a pivotal yet often under-recognized figure in the American civil rights movement. Her relentless dedication to social justice and her ability to empower others exemplify both Grit and Grace.

Early Life and Challenges

Born in 1903 in Norfolk, Virginia, Baker was deeply influenced by her grandmother's stories of slavery and resistance. She pursued higher education at Shaw University, graduating as a valedictorian in 1927. Facing the dual challenges of racial and gender discrimination, Baker committed herself to advocating for marginalized communities.

Demonstrating Grit: Relentless Pursuit of Justice

Baker worked with major civil rights organizations, including the NAACP, the Southern Christian Leadership Conference (SCLC), and the Student Nonviolent Coordinating Committee (SNCC). Her steadfast commitment to grassroots organizing and her belief in collective leadership often put her at odds with more prominent leaders, but she remained undeterred in her mission for equality.

Demonstrating Grace: Empowering Others

Baker's Grace was evident in her approach to leadership. She prioritized listening to and uplifting the voices of ordinary people, especially young activists and women. Her mentorship fostered a new generation of leaders who carried forward the principles of nonviolent resistance and community empowerment.

Legacy of Empowerment: The Power of Grit and Grace

Ella Baker's life is a testament to the enduring impact of combining resilience with empathy. Her behind-the-scenes work laid the foundation for significant civil rights advancements, showing that true leadership often involves empowering others to lead.

Justice Sonia Sotomayor

Sonia Sotomayor, the first Latina Supreme Court Justice in U.S. history, has built a career defined by overcoming adversity to rise through the legal ranks (Grit) and using her platform to advocate for empathy, justice, and inclusivity (Grace). Her journey from a modest upbringing in the Bronx to the highest court in the land is an inspiring testament to perseverance and emotional intelligence.

Early Life and Challenges

Born in 1954 to Puerto Rican parents in a housing project in the Bronx, Sotomayor's childhood was shaped by struggle. Her father died when she was just nine years old, leaving her mother to raise her and her brother alone. To add to the challenge, Sotomayor was diagnosed with Type 1 diabetes as a child, forcing her to develop strict self-discipline at an early age. Despite these hardships, her mother instilled in her a deep respect for education and hard work.

Sotomayor excelled in school, eventually earning a scholarship to Princeton University. As one of the few Latina students there, she initially struggled with self-doubt but refused to let it define her. Instead, she threw herself into her studies, graduating summa cum laude before going on to Yale Law School, where she continued to face skepticism as a Latina in a predominantly white and male field.

Demonstrating Grit: Breaking Barriers in the Legal Field

Sotomayor's grit was clear in her refusal to let barriers stop her. After graduating from Yale, she worked as an assistant district attorney in New York before entering private practice. Her sharp legal mind and unwavering determination led to her appointment as a federal district judge in 1992 and later as an appellate judge.

Her most high-profile moment of resilience came in 2009 when President Barack Obama nominated her to the U.S. Supreme Court. The confirmation process was grueling, with intense scrutiny of her past statements, judicial record, and even her background. Critics questioned whether her identity and life experiences would bias her decisions. Rather than backing down, Sotomayor met the challenge with confidence, articulating her judicial philosophy and defending the importance of diverse perspectives on the bench.

She was confirmed as the first Latina and only the third woman ever to serve on the Supreme Court. Her rise was not due to privilege or connections, but to her relentless determination to succeed despite systemic obstacles.

Demonstrating Grace: Advocating for Empathy and Inclusion

While her grit carried her to the Supreme Court, Sotomayor's grace is seen in how she has used her position to advocate for justice, diversity, and understanding. She has consistently emphasized the importance of empathy in the law, arguing that lived experiences shape how judges interpret cases and understand the impact of their rulings.

Unlike many justices who remain distant from the public, Sotomayor tries to connect with people from all backgrounds. She often visits schools, speaks about the importance of education, and inspires young people—especially Latinos—to pursue their dreams despite adversity. Her memoir, *My Beloved World*, offers a deeply personal reflection on her struggles and triumphs, showing a level of vulnerability and openness that makes her relatable and inspiring.

From the Bronx to the Supreme Court: The Power of Grit and Grace

Sonia Sotomayor's life story exemplifies the balance of grit and grace. Her resilience in overcoming childhood adversity, breaking barriers in the legal profession, and persevering through political scrutiny highlights her mental toughness. At the same time, her compassion, humility, and commitment to lifting others up reflect her emotional intelligence and grace.

As a Supreme Court Justice, she continues to shape American law while serving as a role model for those who face obstacles in their own journeys. Her story is a testament to the idea that true success comes not just from hard work, but from the ability to use one's position to uplift others.

Clara Luper

Clara Luper was a pioneering African American civil rights leader and educator whose courageous actions helped desegregate public spaces in Oklahoma. Her relentless pursuit of equality and her compassionate approach to activism embody both Grit and Grace.

Early Life and Challenges

Born in 1923 in Okfuskee County, Oklahoma, Luper grew up in the segregated South, experiencing firsthand the injustices of racial discrimination. Despite these challenges, she excelled academically, earning a degree in mathematics and later a master's in history education.

Demonstrating Grit: Leading Nonviolent Protests

In 1958, as the advisor for the Oklahoma City NAACP Youth Council, Luper led a group of young students in a sit-in at Katz Drug Store, a segregated lunch counter in Oklahoma City. Facing hostility and threats, their peaceful protest resulted in the desegregation of the establishment, sparking a series of similar protests across the nation.

Demonstrating Grace: Educating and Inspiring Youth

Luper's Grace was evident in her dedication to education and mentorship. As a high school teacher, she inspired countless students to pursue higher education and become active in social justice causes. Her empathetic approach fostered a sense of empowerment among the youth, encouraging them to challenge societal injustices through nonviolent means.

From Segregation to Integration: The Power of Grit and Grace

Clara Luper's unwavering commitment to civil rights and her nurturing guidance of young activists displays the profound impact of combining resilience with empathy. Her legacy continues to inspire future generations to advocate for equality and justice.

Secretary of State Marco Rubio

Marco Rubio, U.S. Senator from Florida and a prominent conservative voice in American politics, has risen from humble beginnings to national leadership through (overcoming financial struggles, setbacks, and political opposition (Grit) and his ability to connect with diverse communities and advocate for the American Dream (Grace). His journey reflects resilience, adaptability, and a deep commitment to public service.

Early Life and Challenges

Born in Miami in 1971 to Cuban immigrants, Rubio's parents came to the U.S. in search of a better life, working as a bartender and housekeeper to support their family. Rubio grew up with a deep understanding of sacrifice and hard work, shaping his belief in the American Dream.

Despite financial hardships, Rubio excelled academically and athletically, earning a football scholarship to Tarkio College in Missouri before transferring to the University of Florida. After completing his undergraduate degree, he went on to earn a law degree from the University of Miami, taking on student debt that he would struggle to pay off early in his political career. These challenges gave him a personal understanding of the struggles many Americans face in achieving financial stability.

Demonstrating Grit: Climbing the Political Ladder Against the Odds

Rubio's political career began at the local level, where he quickly gained recognition for his ambition and policy acumen. In 2000, he was elected to the Florida House of Representatives, eventually becoming Speaker of the House in 2006. His rise was not without challenges—he often had to navigate party divisions, budget battles, and skepticism about his youth and inexperience.

His biggest test of grit came in 2010 when he launched a long shot bid for the U.S. Senate against then-Governor Charlie Crist, who was initially the frontrunner. Despite being outspent and underestimated, Rubio ran an aggressive grassroots campaign, appealing to conservative voters and

Tea Party activists. His perseverance paid off, and he defeated Crist in a stunning upset, becoming one of the youngest U.S. Senators in modern history.

In 2016, Rubio faced another defining moment of resilience when he ran for the Republican presidential nomination. Although he was an early frontrunner, he faced intense competition from Donald Trump and Ted Cruz. His campaign faltered after a difficult debate exchange with Trump, but rather than retreating from politics, Rubio regrouped and successfully won re-election to the Senate. His ability to bounce back from setbacks demonstrates his grit and long-term commitment to public service.

Demonstrating Grace: Connecting with Diverse Communities and Advocating for the American Dream

Rubio's grace is reflected in his ability to connect with people across ideological, generational, and ethnic divides. As a Cuban American, he has often spoken about the immigrant experience, advocating for policies that support economic opportunity and national security while remaining sensitive to the struggles of working-class families.

His approach to leadership has been marked by a willingness to listen, evolve, and build coalitions. On immigration, for example, he initially supported comprehensive reform efforts but shifted his stance in response to political realities. Although controversial, this adaptability showcases his ability to balance principle with pragmatism.

Rubio has also shown grace in his personal and public interactions, keeping composure in the face of criticism and engaging in thoughtful discourse even with political opponents. His speeches often emphasize optimism, faith, and unity, reflecting a deep belief in the potential of the American people.

From a Working-Class Immigrant Family to the U.S. Senate and the U.S. Secretary of State: The Power of Grit and Grace

Marco Rubio's journey—from the son of working-class immigrants to a national leader—exemplifies the power of grit and grace. His resilience in overcoming financial hardships, electoral challenges, and political adversity has shaped his career, while his empathy and ability to inspire have made him a respected voice in American politics.

Whether shaping economic policies, championing human rights, or fostering connections across diverse communities, Rubio's journey exemplifies that true success extends beyond ambition—it requires the ability to listen, connect, and lead with conviction and grace. His steadfast commitment to balancing resilience and diplomacy throughout his career culminated in a remarkable moment of unity when a deeply divided Senate confirmed him as Secretary of State with a unanimous 99-0 vote on January 20, 2025. This rare display of bipartisan support not only affirmed his qualifications but also underscored the enduring impact of grit and grace in leadership.

The True Source of Grit and Grace

After completing the manuscript for this book, I couldn't shake the feeling that something was missing. How could this be? I had worked hard to ensure it was filled with rich content—frameworks, tools, examples, and personal stories that illuminate the path of Grit and Grace. I had drawn from research, life experience, and the lives of extraordinary individuals to offer what I believed was a complete picture. But even after multiple readings, edits, and revisions, something still felt incomplete.

Despite that lingering tension, I moved forward. I submitted the manuscript to my editor, engaged a designer for the cover, and pressed on toward the deadlines. Yet for weeks—months, even—the uneasiness persisted. I would lie awake at night with a vague but persistent sense that the book, though accurate and useful, wasn't *whole*.

So, I did what I often do when I am in need of wisdom ... I prayed ... not for inspiration in the usual sense, but for clarity. As a person of faith, I believe that wisdom often arrives not with fanfare, but with a whisper. I didn't receive a thunderbolt of revelation. What I did receive, slowly and quietly, was a deepening conviction:

The truth is, I am not the ultimate authority on Grit and Grace.

Yes, I've lived these concepts. I've studied them, taught them, coached others in them. But the deepest source of these qualities—the place where grit is born and grace is sustained—is not something I can claim as my own, nor can the authors and researches I've cited throughout this book. The missing piece was not a new tool, an inspiring new story, or another quote. It was the acknowledgment of where these strengths ultimately originate

At the heart of this journey—this exploration of Grit and Grace—is a deeper truth that has anchored my life and shaped the very lens through which I see resilience, empathy, leadership, and growth. It is the truth that we were created not to walk alone, nor to strive by our own strength alone, but to live in relationship with a loving and sovereign God who equips us, refines us, and sustains us.

The pursuit of mental toughness and emotional intelligence—what I've called Grit and Grace—can be deeply enriched when viewed through the lens of the Holy Scriptures. In fact, the Bible is filled with examples of individuals who exemplified these very traits, not through personal ambition or human willpower alone, but through a reliance on God's power, purpose, and promises.

Real Grit is rooted in a divine purpose.

Isaiah reminds us, *"But those who wait upon the Lord shall renew their strength; they shall mount up with wings like eagles, they shall run and not be weary, they shall walk and not faint"* (Isaiah 40:31). That kind of endurance is not born from grit alone—it is born from divine dependence.

Consider Paul, whose perseverance in the face of prison, persecution, and shipwreck was not mere stubborn resolve, but Spirit-empowered grit. *"I press on to take hold of that for which Christ Jesus took hold of me,"* he writes in Philippians 3:12. He wasn't chasing self-actualization—he was pursuing a holy calling.

Real Grace flows from the heart of God.

On the other side of the coin, James exhorts believers to be *"quick to listen, slow to speak, and slow to become angry"* (James 1:19)—a clear directive to cultivate grace in our interactions.

The emotional intelligence we strive for in leadership and relationships has its deepest roots in the humility and wisdom modeled by Christ Himself.

Jesus, the perfect embodiment of both grit and grace, showed unwavering determination in fulfilling His purpose—culminating in the Cross. And yet, He consistently led with compassion, restored the broken, forgave the unforgivable, and extended dignity to the outcast. His life and teachings are the ultimate guide to leading with both strength and empathy. *"Come to me, all you who are weary and burdened, and I will give you rest,"* Jesus invites us in Matthew 11:28. That's grace. And it's offered freely, not earned. It is through that grace that we are empowered to extend it to others.

Paul reminds us of this divine assignment in 2 Corinthians 5:20: *"We are therefore Christ's ambassadors, as though God were making His appeal through us."* As His representatives, we are called not only to declare the truth but to demonstrate it through our conduct—through grace-filled conversations, empathetic leadership, and unwavering integrity. To live out grit and grace is to live as ambassadors of Christ in a world that desperately needs both courage and compassion.

The true source for a life of Grit and Grace is a relationship with God.

The wisdom literature offers yet another guiding thread. Proverbs reminds us that, *"The heart of man plans his way, but the Lord establishes his steps"* (Proverbs 16:9). Grit may get us moving. Grace may guide our manner. But it is God who charts the course and brings purpose to the journey.

Psalm 37:5 echoes this assurance: *"Commit your way to the Lord; trust in Him, and He will act."* Trust. Obedience. Humility. These are the virtues beneath the surface of mental toughness and emotional intelligence. They are the soil in which Grit and Grace grow.

And so, as I close this book, I offer not just a framework for personal and professional development—but an invitation to a deeper transformation. One that goes beyond behavior into the soul. One that invites the reader to anchor their Grit in God's strength, and to extend Grace from the overflow of His love.

May your life be marked by relentless purpose and radical compassion. May you lead with courage and kindness. And may you remember that the ultimate source of true Grit and Grace is not found in you—but in the One who created you, redeemed you, and calls you forward.

"He has shown you, O man, what is good. And what does the Lord require of you? To act justly, and to love mercy, and to walk humbly with your God." — Micah 6:8

If, after reading this, you feel a sense of "calling" to explore this transformation, this personal relationship with our Creator, please reach out to me. It would be an honor to discuss it more fully with you.

All the Best to you in Work, in Family, in Faith, and in Life.

Jeff

(www.JeffStandridge.com)

Grit and Grace Self-Assessment

For each statement, rate yourself on a scale from 1 to 5, using the following scale:

5 = Strongly Agree * 4 = Agree * 3 = Neutral
2 = Disagree * 1 = Strongly Disagree

1	I remain committed to my goals, even in the face of obstacles and setbacks.	
2	I am aware of my emotions and how they can affect my thoughts and behavior.	
3	I view challenges as opportunities to grow and learn.	
4	I have a good understanding of the emotions of people around me.	
5	I can keep my emotions in check when things do not go as planned.	
6	I can manage my emotions, even in stressful situations.	
7	I often find ways to persevere when others would give up.	
8	I am skilled at resolving conflicts in a way that satisfies all parties.	
9	I believe I can overcome most of the difficulties I face.	
10	I can communicate my feelings effectively and listen empathetically to others.	
11	I can recover quickly from emotional distress.	

12	I actively look to improve my ability to empathize with others.	
13	My dedication to my goals persists, regardless of external criticism or doubt.	
14	I can accurately identify others' emotions, even when they are not openly expressed.	
15	I adapt and find new ways to achieve my goals when faced with setbacks.	
16	I have strategies in place for regulating my emotions in professional settings.	
17	I am constantly reflecting on past challenges to build my resilience.	
18	I prioritize understanding others' perspectives in a conflict.	
19	My motivation is internal and not easily swayed by outside forces.	
20	I maintain emotional balance, even in situations of personal criticism.	

Total Score for Questions
1,3,5,7,9,11,13,15,17,19: ______ /50 = ______ (Grit Score)

Total Score for Questions
2,4,6,8,10,12,14,16,18,20: ______ /50 = _______ (Grace Score)

Total Combined Score: _________ **(Balance Between Grit and Grace)**

Interpretation Key:

In each area (Grit and Grace)

<u>Total Score</u>

0 - 25 (Low):	Critical development is needed.
26 - 40 (Moderate)	Good foundation, but there is room for improvement.
41 - 50 (High):	Strong skills are present in both areas.

Potential Improvement Prescriptions for Mental Toughness/Grit:

If your score is between 10-25 (Low):

You may often find it hard to push through challenges and maintain your momentum toward your goals when faced with adversity. Consider the following suggestions to boost your mental toughness, resilience, and grit:

1. **Set Clear, Achievable Goals:** Break down your big goals into smaller, manageable tasks to avoid feeling overwhelmed.
2. **Embrace Challenges:** View each challenge as an opportunity to grow. Start with small challenges and work your way up.
3. **Develop Emotional Regulation:** Practice mindfulness or stress-reduction techniques to help manage your emotions during trying times.
4. **Seek Feedback:** Learn from criticism rather than being discouraged by it. Seek feedback from trusted mentors or peers.
5. **Reflect on Past Successes:** Spend time reflecting on situations where you have overcome obstacles in the past. This can increase your belief in your ability to handle future challenges.
6. **Surround Yourself with Support:** Build a network of supportive friends or colleagues who can offer advice and encouragement.

If your score is between 26-40 (Moderate):

You have shown some capability in dealing with challenges and staying committed to your goals, but there's room for growth. To enhance your mental toughness, consider:

1. **Refine Goal setting:** Make sure your goals are specific, measurable, achievable, relevant, and time-bound (SMART).
2. **Cultivate a Growth Mindset:** Foster a belief that your abilities can be developed through dedication and hard work.
3. **Practice Persistence:** Deliberately put yourself in situations that require perseverance. Small practices in persistence can build your resilience over time.
4. **Focus On What You Can Control:** Direct your energy toward your reaction and approach to obstacles instead of dwelling on the barriers themselves.
5. **Celebrate Small Wins:** Acknowledge and celebrate your progress, even if it is minimal. This can boost your motivation.

If your score is between 41-50 (High):

You already exhibit a high level of mental toughness, resilience, and grit. To further enhance these qualities, focus on:

1. **Seek New Challenges:** Constantly look for new challenges that push you out of your comfort zone and foster growth.
2. **Mentor Others:** Sharing your experiences and guiding others in developing their mental toughness can reinforce your own skills and offer new insights.
3. **Continue Self-reflection:** Even if you are reflecting on challenges regularly, delve deeper into your thought processes and emotions to uncover new areas of improvement.
4. **Strengthen Emotional Intelligence:** Working on understanding and managing your emotions can provide a solid foundation for mental toughness in varied situations.

Potential Improvement Prescriptions for Emotional Intelligence/Grace

If your score is between 10-25 (Low)

1. **Develop Self-Awareness:** Start a daily journal focusing on your emotions, noting what triggered these feelings, how you reacted, and how you might handle it differently next time. This practice can enhance your awareness of your emotions and their impact.
2. **Learn to Recognize Others' Emotions:** Pay more attention to body language, facial expressions, and tone of voice in your daily interactions. Consider their perspective and context to better understand their emotions.
3. **Practice Stress Management:** Develop a list of strategies that help you calm down when stressed, such as deep breathing exercises, meditation, or physical activity. Experiment to find what works best for you.
4. **Enhance Communication Skills:** Work on expressing your feelings in a constructive manner and practice active listening. Consider joining a communication skills workshop or a public speaking group like Toastmasters.
5. **Seek Feedback:** Ask trusted friends, family members, or colleagues for feedback on your emotional responses and conflict resolution skills. Be open to their observations and suggestions.

If your score is between 26-40 (Moderate)

1. **Boost Emotional Regulation:** Challenge negative thoughts and reframe them in a more positive or realistic way. This cognitive restructuring can help in managing emotions more effectively.
2. **Expand Emotional Vocabulary:** Enhance your ability to express and identify emotions by learning new emotion-related words. This can improve your communication in emotional situations.
3. **Conflict Resolution Skills:** Practice empathy in conflicts by actively trying to see the situation from the other person's perspective. Seek win-win solutions where all parties feel heard and respected.
4. **Empathetic Listening:** Focus on really hearing what the other person is saying without planning your response. Reflect back what you have heard to ensure understanding.
5. **Mindfulness Practices:** Incorporate mindfulness or meditation into your daily routine to improve your emotional balance and presence in the moment.

If your score is between 41-50 (High)

1. **Continued Learning:** Even with strong EI skills, there is always room to grow. Attend workshops or read books on emotional intelligence, communication, and leadership.
2. **Mentor Others:** Share your emotional intelligence skills by mentoring others. This can also be a powerful way to reflect on and enhance your own abilities.
3. **Volunteer for Challenging Projects:** Look for opportunities that challenge your emotional intelligence, such as projects involving cross-functional teams or roles requiring negotiation and conflict resolution.
4. **Reflect and Refine:** Regularly reflect on emotional experiences to continuously refine your strategies and approaches. Consider how different strategies work in varying contexts.
5. **Build a Support Network:** Engage with a network of emotionally intelligent peers for mutual learning and support. Sharing experiences and insights can further your growth.

Remember, improving emotional intelligence is a journey, not a destination. Regularly reassess your progress by retaking this self-evaluation and adjusting your strategies as needed.

The Grit Workout

Grit is the combination of passion and perseverance for long-term goals. It is about sticking with your commitments, pushing through challenges, and staying focused even when things get tough. In this workout, we will explore how you can cultivate grit in your own life, build resilience, and achieve your goals more effectively.

1. **Before diving into exercises to build grit or grace, it is essential to understand where you currently stand. Begin by assessing yourself using the "Grit and Grace Assessment" above.**

Grit involves staying committed to long-term goals. In this section, you will learn how to set goals that are challenging yet realistic and aligned with your core values.

2. **List one-to-three long-term goals using the SMART framework (Specific, Measurable, Achievable, Relevant, Time-bound).**

- **Specific:** What exactly do you want to achieve?
- **Measurable:** How will you know you are making progress?
- **Achievable:** Is the goal realistic given your resources?
- **Relevant:** Does this goal align with your values and priorities?
- **Time-bound:** What is your deadline for reaching this goal?

3. **Reflect on a time when you set a long-term goal and stuck with it despite challenges. What factors helped you stay committed?**

Resilience is a core component of grit. It is about bouncing back from setbacks and maintaining motivation when things get tough.

4. **Identify a challenge or setback you have recently faced. Answer the following questions:**

a. *What was the setback?*
b. *How did you initially react?*
c. *What strategies did you use to overcome it?*
d. *What did you learn from the experience?*

5. **List three strategies you can use to stay resilient in the face of future challenges.**

Grit involves consistent effort over time. Here, you will work on building daily habits that align with your goals.

6. **Identify one habit you need to develop to reach your goals. Track your progress for thirty days.**

How does focusing on small daily actions contribute to your long-term success? What challenges do you face in staying consistent?

Everyone encounters obstacles on the road to success. This section will help you identify potential roadblocks and develop strategies to overcome them.

7. **For each goal you have set, list potential obstacles and brainstorm solutions.**

    - Goal:
    - Obstacle:
    - Solution:

8. **Think of a time when you faced a significant obstacle in the past.**

    How did you overcome it?

    What role did grit play in helping you push through?

Persistence is the backbone of grit. It is about staying the course even when motivation wanes.

9. **When you want to give up, it is often because you have lost sight of your "why." Use the Five Whys technique to dig deeper into your motivation.**

a. *Why is this goal important to you?*
b. *Why does that reason matter?*
c. *Why is that significant?*
d. *Why does that align with your values?*
e. *Why will achieving this goal make a difference in your life?*

Reflect on a situation where persistence paid off. What kept you going, and what did you learn about your ability to persevere?

A growth mindset is essential for developing grit. It is the belief that your abilities can improve with effort and learning.

10. **Read the following statements and decide whether they reflect a growth mindset or a fixed mindset.**

- "I'm not good at this, so I won't even try."
- "I can get better with practice."
- "Challenges are opportunities to learn."
- "Failure means I'm not cut out for this."

How can adopting a growth mindset help you build more grit?

What areas of your life would benefit from this shift in perspective?

Long-term goals require sustained motivation. In this section, you will explore techniques to stay motivated even when progress is slow.

11. **For seven days, write down what motivates you each morning. Include quotes, affirmations, or visualizations that inspire you.**

What patterns do you notice in what motivates you?

How can you use this awareness to keep pushing forward?

It is important to regularly assess how far you have come and where you still need to grow.

12. **Set aside time each month to reflect on your progress using the following questions:**

    - *What wins have I had this month?*
    - *What setbacks did I face, and how did I handle them?*
    - *Where do I need to focus my efforts next?*

How has your grit evolved since you began this workbook?

What are the biggest changes you have noticed in your mindset, habits, and perseverance?

Developing grit is not a one-time achievement; it is a lifelong process. By consistently applying the exercises and reflections in this workbook, you will build the resilience, determination, and persistence needed to achieve your goals. Remember that setbacks are part of the journey, and the most important thing is to keep moving forward with passion and perseverance.

13. **How will you continue to practice grit in your daily life?**

14. **What commitments can you make to yourself today to ensure that you stay on track?**

The Grace Workout

Grace is more than just kindness—it is the embodiment of emotional intelligence, empathy, and the ability to maintain relationships even in challenging times. It is about leading with compassion, listening with intent, and navigating life with an understanding heart. This workout is designed to help you build and apply the elements of grace, enhancing both your personal and professional relationships.

Understanding your own emotions is the first step in developing grace. When you are self-aware, you are better equipped to manage your reactions and connect with others.

1. **Spend five minutes each morning and evening asking yourself the following questions:**

a. What emotions am I feeling right now?
b. What triggered these emotions?
c. How am I responding to these emotions—positively or negatively?

How does your emotional state affect your interactions with others?

In what ways can improving your self-awareness help you respond more gracefully?

Empathy is the ability to understand and share the feelings of others.

It is the foundation of grace, allowing you to connect with others on a deeper level.

2. **Choose one conversation each day where your goal is simply to listen.**
   Don't interrupt, give advice, or offer your opinion. Focus entirely on understanding the other person's perspective.

What did you learn from this exercise about the power of listening?

How did it change the dynamics of the conversation?

Grace in action means fostering relationships built on trust, mutual respect, and open communication.

3. **Identify three key relationships in your life (personal or professional).**

For each relationship, note one action you can take this week to strengthen trust. Examples might include being more transparent, offering help without being asked, or simply expressing appreciation.

What changes did you notice in these relationships after taking intentional steps to build trust? How can you continue to nurture these connections?

Part of showing grace is managing your emotions in stressful or triggering situations.

Emotional regulation helps you respond thoughtfully rather than reacting impulsively.

4. **Whenever you feel a strong emotion rising, pause before responding.**

Count to ten, take a deep breath, and ask yourself: "What response would be the most constructive and compassionate in this situation?"

In what situations do you find it most difficult to pause and regulate your emotions?

How did using the pause technique change the outcome of your interactions?

Grace is rooted in acts of compassion and kindness, both toward others and yourself.

5. **For one week, perform one small act of kindness each day.**

It could be a compliment, a supportive note, or helping someone in need. Record what you did and how it made you feel.

How did focusing on kindness influence your mood and outlook?

What impact did these small acts have on your relationships?

When faced with stress or conflict, grace helps you stay calm, composed, and empathetic.

6. **Think of a recent conflict where emotions ran high.**

   Write about how you handled it, then rewrite the scenario imagining how you could have responded with more grace.

a. *What triggered the conflict?*
b. *How did you initially react?*
c. *How could you have approached the situation differently?*
d. *What could you do next time to bring more empathy and understanding?*

What did you learn from analyzing past conflicts?
How can grace change the way you approach difficult conversations?

Grace does not mean saying yes to everything.
Healthy boundaries are essential for preserving your well-being and protecting your energy.

7. **Identify one area in your life where you need to set or reinforce a boundary.**

8. **Develop a plan for how you will communicate this boundary with respect and clarity.**

How did setting boundaries affect your stress levels and your relationships?

What challenges did you face in maintaining those boundaries?

Graceful communication balances assertiveness with empathy.

It is about expressing your needs while considering the feelings of others.

9. **Identify a situation where you need to express your needs or opinions assertively. Plan how you will communicate in a way that is both clear and compassionate. Practice using "I" statements (i.e., "I feel... when...").**

How did assertiveness combined with empathy improve the outcome of your communication? What did you learn about balancing strength with grace?

Grace is a journey, not a destination. Regular reflection helps you track your progress and stay committed to living with empathy and compassion.

10. **At the end of each month, take time to reflect on how you have grown in grace.**

    Use these prompts to guide your reflection:

a. *What situations challenged your ability to show grace this month?*
b. *How did you respond with empathy and compassion?*
c. *What have you learned about yourself and others?*
d. *What actions will you take next month to continue growing in grace?*

What has been the most notable change in how you approach relationships and challenges since you began focusing on grace? How can you sustain this growth?

Living with grace is about showing empathy, emotional intelligence, and a heart for others—even in the most demanding situations. As you continue your journey, remember that grace is both an inner strength and an outward expression. It is the kindness you show to others, the patience you offer yourself, and the calm presence you bring to every interaction.

11. **How will you carry the principles of grace into your daily life moving forward?**

12. **What commitments can you make today to lead with more empathy and understanding?**

References

Abramson, A. (2022, January 1). *Burnout and stress are everywhere.* Retrieved from American Psychological Association: https://www.apa.org/monitor/2022/01/special-burnout-stress

Abu-Tineh, A. M., Khasawneh, S. A., & Al-Omari, A. A. (2009). Kouzes and Posner's transformational leadership model in practice: The case of Jordanian schools. *Journal of Leadership Education*, *7*(3), 265–283.

Ackerman, C. E. (2018, July 3). What is Self-Regulation? (+95 Skills and Strategies). PositivePsychology.com. https://positivepsychology.com/self-regulation/

Akhtar, N., Sajjad, N., & Khattak, S. R. (2014). Impact of Emotional Intelligence on Career Decision Making Self Efficacy among Students of Pakistani Universities. NUML Journal of Management & Technology, *9*(1).

Baker, C. (2023, March 22). *Emotional Intelligence in the Workplace: What You Should Know.* Retrieved from Leaders: https://leaders.com/articles/personal-growth/emotional-intelligence-in-the-workplace/

Bakker, Arnold, & Bal, Matthijs, (2010). Journal of occupational and organizational psychology. Bakker, Arnold; Bal, Matthijs. (2010). Weekly work engagement and performance: A study among starting teachers. Journal of

Occupational and Organizational Psychology, 83 (1), Reino Unido. (pp. 189–206). https://doi. org/10.1348/096317909X402596, *83*(1)), 189–209.

Bariso, J. (2024, March 28). *His Teammate Got Ejected for Cursing at a Referee. Stephen Curry's Response Is a* Brilliant Lesson in Emotional Intelligence. Retrieved from Inc.: https://www.inc.com/justin-bariso/his-teammate-got-ejected-for-cursing-at-a-referee-steph-currys-response-is-a-brilliant-lesson-in-emotional-intelligence.html

Bariso, J. (2016, October 25). *Steph Curry's Inspiring New Commercial Teaches a Lesson in Emotional Intelligence.* Retrieved from Inc.: https://www.inc.com/justin-bariso/steph-currys-inspiring-new-commercial-teaches-a-lesson-in-emotional-intelligence.html

Bar-On, R. (2006). The Bar-On model of emotional-social intelligence (ESI). Psicothema, 18 (supl.), 13–25.

Baumeister, R. F., & Tierney, J. (2011). Willpower: Rediscovering the Greatest Human Strength. Penguin Press.

Beckett, J. D. (2006). Loving Monday: Succeeding In Business Without Selling Your Soul. InterVarsity Press.

Borins, S., & Herst, B. (2018). Cults of Personality: Fables of the Automobile Manufacturing Industry. Negotiating Business Narratives: Fables of the Information Technology, Automobile Manufacturing, and Financial Trading Industries, 23–35.

Boehmer, E. (2008). Nelson Mandela: A very short introduction. Oxford University Press.

Brackett, Marc. (2006). *Measuring emotional intelligence with the Mayer-Salovery-Caruso Emotional Intelligence Test (MSCEIT).* Retrieved from Psicothema: https://www.psicothema.com/pdf/3273.pdf

Brown, B. (2018). Dare to Lead: Brave Work. Tough Conversations. Whole Hearts. Random House.

Brown, T., & Katz, B. (2019). Change by Design: How Design Thinking Transforms Organizations and Inspires Innovation. Harper Business.

Craig, H. (2019, January 30). *The Theories of Emotional Intelligence Explained.* Retrieved from Positive Psychology: https://positivepsychology.com/emotional-intelligence-theories/

Carlin, J. (2008). Playing the enemy: Nelson Mandela and the game that made a nation. Penguin Books.

Catmull, E., & Wallace, A. (2014). Creativity Inc.: Overcoming the Unseen Forces That Stand in the Way of True Inspiration. Random House.

Catmull, E. (2008, September). How Pixar Fosters Collective Creativity. Harvard Business Review. https://hbr.org/2008/09/how-pixar-fosters-collective-creativity

Cherry, K. (2022, December 11). *Utilizing Emotional Intelligence in the Workplace.* Retrieved from VeryWell Mind: https://www.verywellmind.com/utilizing-emotional-intelligence-in-the-workplace-4164713

Chirumbolo, A., Picconi, L., Morelli, M., & Petrides, K. V. (2019). The Assessment of Trait Emotional Intelligence: Psychometric Characteristics of the TEIQue-Full Form in a Large Italian Adult Sample. Frontiers in Psychology,

9. https://doi.org/10.3389/fpsyg.2018.02786

Churchill, W. (1940). Never Give In: The Best of Winston Churchill's Speeches. Pimlico.

Clear, J. (2018). Atomic Habits: An Easy & Proven Way to Build Good Habits & Break Bad Ones. Avery.

Clough, P., Earle, K., & Sewell, D. (2002). Mental toughness: The concept and its measurement. In I. Cockerill (Ed.), *Solutions in sport psychology* (pp. 32–43). Thomson Learning.

Clough, P., Earle, K., & Strycharczyk, D. (2015). Developing Mental Toughness: Improving Performance, Wellbeing and *Positive* Behaviour in Others. Kogan Page Publishers.

Covey, S. R., & Merrill, R. R. (2008). *The SPEED of Trust: The One Thing That Changes Everything.* Simon and *Schuster.*

Covey, S. R. (1989). The 7 Habits of Highly Effective People: Powerful Lessons in Personal Change. Free Press.

Covey, S. R. (1991). *The seven habits of highly effective people.* Provo, UT: Covey Leadership Center.

Cowden, R. G. (2016). Mental Toughness, Emotional Intelligence, and Coping Effectiveness. Perceptual and Motor Skills, 123(3), *737*–753. https://doi.org/10.1177/0031512516666027

Daily Inspired Life. (2023). Real-Life Stories of Resilience to Empower You Through Adversity. Retrieved from https://www.dailyinspiredlife.com

DeVitis, J. L., & Rich, J. M. (1996). The Success Ethic, Education, and the American Dream. SUNY Press.

Desai, K. (2024). Empathy – A key component of Emotional Intelligence. Linkedin.com. https://www.linkedin.com/pulse/empathy-key-component-emotional-intelligence-kalpan-desai/

Druskat, V. U., & Kayes, D. C. (2000). The impact of emotional intelligence on team performance. Journal of Applied Psychology, *85*(6), 935–944.

Duckworth, A. L. (2016). Grit: The Power of Passion and Perseverance. Scribner.

Dweck, C. S. (2006). Mindset: The New Psychology of Success. Ballantine Books.

Edmondson, A. C. (2019). The Fearless Organization: Creating Psychological Safety in the Workplace for Learning, Innovation, and Growth. John Wiley & Sons.

Fugère, M. A. (2021). College students in the western world are becoming less emotionally intelligent: A cross-temporal meta-analysis of trait emotional intelligence. Psychology Today. https://www.psychologytoday.com/us/blog/the-science-attraction/why-emotional-intelligence-is-declining

Gharib, A. (2023, November 23). Dell, Stephen and Seth Curry top NBA father-son duos - ESPN. ESPN; ESPN. https://www.espn.in/nba/story/_/id/38955259/nba-top-father-son-duos-walton-thompson-curry-sabonis

Google. (2023). *Team dynamics: The five keys to building effective teams*. Think with Google. https://www.thinkwithgoogle.com/

Goleman, D. (2015). *Emotional Intelligence (EQ).* Journal of K, 6, 71–77.

Goleman, D. (2009). Working with Emotional Intelligence. A&C Black.

Goleman, D., Boyatzis, R., & McKee, A. (2002). Primal leadership: Realizing the power of emotional intelligence. Harvard Business School Press.

Goleman, D. (1998). What makes a leader? Harvard Business Review, *76*(6), 93–102.

Goleman, D. (1995). Emotional Intelligence: Why It Can Matter More Than IQ. Bantam Books.

Gunaydin, H. M. (2006). *The Delphi Method.* Optimization Group.

Guy-Evans, O., Mcleod, S. (2024, February 5). How To Improve Emotional Intelligence. Simply Psychology. https://www.simplypsychology.org/how-to-improve-emotional-intelligence.html

Haley. (n.d.). *5 Ways to Promote Resilience Through Exercise.* Retrieved from Fitness Blender: https://www.fitnessblender.com/articles/5-ways-to-promote-resilience-through-exercise

Hanford, E. (n.d.). *Angela Duckworth and the Research on 'Grit'.* Retrieved from American Public Media: https://americanradioworks.publicradio.org/features/tomorrows-college/grit/angela-duckworth-grit.html

Hayrettin Gumusdag. (2023). Examination of Mental Toughness in Sports Teams. ASEAN Journal of Psychiatry, *24*(10). https://doi.org/10.54615/2231-7805.47333

Heath, C., & Heath, D. (2010). Switch: How to Change Things When Change Is Hard. Broadway Books.

Hill, N. (2015). *Think and Grow Rich: The Original Version, Restored and Revised™.* SCB Distributors.

Hill, N. (1937). Think and Grow Rich. The Ralston Society.

Hoffner, E. (2023, September 5). "In business to save the planet," Patagonia says people & planet should be the priority of corporations. Mongabay Environmental News. https://news.mongabay.com/2023/09/in-business-to-save-the-planet-patagonia-says-corporations-should-prioritize-people-planet/

Isaacson, W. (2011). Steve Jobs. Simon & Schuster.

Khan, M., Minbashian, A., & MacCann, C. (2021) College students in the western world are becoming less emotionally intelligent: A cross-temporal meta-analysis of trait emotional intelligence. *Journal of Personality.* https://doi.org/10.1111/jopy.12643

Kelley, R. E. (1998). How to Be a Star at Work: Nine Breakthrough Strategies You Need to Succeed. Crown Business.

Kishore, K. (2020, May 14). Examples Of Emotional Intelligence. Harappa. https://harappa.education/harappa-diaries/examples-of-emotional-intelligence-in-the-workplace/

Korn Ferry Institute. (2023). Is emotional intelligence on the decline? Korn Ferry. https://www.kornferry.com/insights/briefings-magazine/emotional-intelligence-decline

Kouzes, J. M., & Posner, B. Z. (2010). *The Five Practices of Exemplary Leadership* (Vol. 237). John Wiley & Sons.

Kouzes, J. M., & Posner, B. Z. (1987). The Leadership Challenge: How to Make Extraordinary Things Happen in Organizations. Jossey-Bass.

Leyshon, J. (2020). *Psychological safety: The secret to Google's top teams' success – and 5 lessons for workplaces*. Sage Advice UK. https://www.sage.com/

Li, S. (2022). The Relationship Between Mental Toughness and Academic Achievement and Its Relevant Factors. Proceedings *of the 2022 8th International Conference on Humanities and Social Science Research (ICHSSR 2022).* Los Angeles, California: Atlantis Press.

Luca, J., & Tarricone, P. (2001). Does emotional intelligence affect successful teamwork? (pp. 9–12). https://ro.ecu.edu.au/cgi/viewcontent.cgi?article=5833&context=ecuworks

Mahoney, J. W., Gucciardi, D. F., Ntoumanis, N., & Mallett, C. J. (2014). The development of the Mental Toughness Inventory (MTI): A comprehensive psychometric examination of the construct. *Personality and Individual Differences*, 69, 102–107. https://doi.org/10.1016/j.paid.2014.05.013

Mandela, N. (1994). Long walk to freedom: The autobiography of Nelson

Mandela. Little, Brown and Company.

Mayer, J. D., Salovey, P., & Caruso, D. R. (2002). Mayer-Salovey-Caruso Emotional Intelligence Test (MSCEIT) User's Manual. Multi-Health Systems Inc.

McChrystal, S. A., Collins, T., Silverman, D., & Fussell, C. (2015). Team of Teams: New Rules of Engagement for a Complex World. Portfolio.

Mayer, J. D., Caruso, D. R., & Salovey, P. (2016). The ability model of emotional intelligence: Principles and updates. Emotion Review, *8*(4), 290–300. https://doi.org/10.1177/1754073916639667

Meraz, R. (2024). Mental Strength: 7 ways to develop mental fortitude and build resilience | Zella Life. Zellalife.com. https://www.zellalife.com/blog/mental-fortitude/

Mental Toughness and Tenacity. (2022, August 27). Retrieved from Walter Wendler: https://walterwendler.com/2022/08/mental-toughness-and-tenacity/

Middleton, S. C. (2007). Mental Toughness: Conceptualisation and Measurement (Doctoral dissertation, University of Western Sydney).

Miller, W. R., & Rollnick, S. (2013). Motivational Interviewing: Helping People Change (3rd ed.). Guilford Press.

Nadella, S. (2017). Hit Refresh: The Quest to Rediscover Microsoft's Soul and Imagine a Better Future for Everyone. Harper Business.

Nguyen, T. H. (2023). *Impact of Emotional Intelligence on Employees' Job Performance: A Case Study of FPT* Telecom *Joint Stock Company.* Hanoi, Vietnam: Atlantis Press.

O'Byrne, C. (2023, June 15). *7 Powerful Strategies to Cultivate Mental Toughness.* Retrieved from LinkedIn: https://www.linkedin.com/pulse/7-powerful-strategies-cultivate-mental-toughness-chris-o-byrne/

Opre. (2023). Resilient Leadership: Cultivating Emotional Intelligence and Mental Toughness. Retrieved from https://www.getopre.com

Penrod, O. (2010). Digital Commons @Georgia Southern Army Continuing Education System: The Role of Emotional Intelligence in Army Education Leadership as It Pertains to Team Performance. https://digitalcommons.georgiasouthern.edu/cgi/viewcontent.cgi?article=1318&context=etd

Petrides, K. V., & Furnham, A. (2001). Trait emotional intelligence: Psychometric investigation with reference to established trait taxonomies. European Journal of Personality, *15*(6), 425–448. https://doi.org/10.1002/per.416

Petrides, K. V. (2009). Technical manual for the Trait Emotional Intelligence

Questionnaires (TEIQue). London Psychometric Laboratory.

Porter, S. (2023, August 23). *Stress Inoculation Training: Definition, Techniques, & What to Expect.* Retrieved from Choosing Therapy: https://www.choosingtherapy.com/stress-inoculation-training/

Rashid, F., Edmondson, A. C., & Leonard, H. B. (2013, July). Leadership Lessons from the Chilean Mine Rescue. Harvard Business Review. https://hbr.org/2013/07/leadership-lessons-from-the-chilean-mine-rescue

Ray, J. (2023, June 27). *Global Rise in Unhappiness Stalls.* Retrieved from Gallup: https://news.gallup.com/poll/507725/global-rise-unhappiness-stalls.aspx

Rhode, D. L. (2017). Leadership in law. Stanford Law Review, *69*(6), 1603.

Roach, K. N. (2023). *Leveraging Grit in Military Research: A Comprehensive Review.* Fort Belvoir, Virginia: United States Army Research Institute for the Behavioral and Social Sciences.

Rostami, R., & Mohammadi, N. (2022). A Comparative Study on Emotional Intelligence and Mental Toughness for Visually Impaired Male and Female Athletes. International Journal of Kinesiology and Sports Science, *3*(4), 74–78. https://journals.aiac.org.au/index.php/IJKSS/article/view/2040

Sampson, A. (1999). Mandela: The authorized biography. HarperCollins.

Saunders, T. (1996). *The Effect of Stress Inoculation Training on Anxiety and Performance.* Winter Park, FL: U.S Army Research Institute for the Behavioral and Social Sciences.

Sean Robson, T. M. (2014). *Enhancing Performance Under Stress.* Santa Monica, California: RAND Corporation.

Sports Visualization: The Secret Weapon of Athletes. (n.d.). Retrieved from Peak Performance Sports: https://www.peaksports.com/sports-psychology-blog/sports-visualization-athletes/

Sprakties, M. A. (2023, May 5). *Grit: A Necessary Trait to Ensure Success in Future Operating Environments.* Retrieved from The Havok Journal: https://havokjournal.com/culture/military/grit-a-necessary-trait-to-ensure-success-in-future-operating-environments/

Stress: statistics. (2018). Retrieved from Mental Health Foundation: https://www.mentalhealth.org.uk/explore-mental-health/statistics/stress-statistics

Sinek, S. (2009). Start With Why: How Great Leaders Inspire Everyone to Take Action. Portfolio.

Sinek, S. (2014). Leaders Eat Last: Why Some Teams Pull Together and Others

Don't. Portfolio.

Six Seconds. (2024). State of the heart: 2024 report. Six Seconds. https://www.6seconds.org/

Shuman, C. (2021). Emotional intelligence can improve resilience. Psychology Today. https://www.psychologytoday.com/us/articles/emotional-intelligence-can-improve-resilience

Standridge, J. (2023). Developing Mental Toughness: A Perfect 10 For People Who Win. AMP. Retrieved from: https://armoneyandpolitics.com/mental-toughness-jeff/

Standridge, J., & Autrey, S. (2001). Rapid Skill Obsolescence in an IT Company: A Case Study of Acxiom Corporation. Journal of Organizational Excellence.

Standridge J. (1999). In search of the professional: modeling the successful respiratory care practitioners of the 21st century. A core competency model [dissertation]. University of Arkansas at Little Rock.

Strycharczyk, D. (2021, October 8). Developing mental toughness in leadership and why it matters. Viewpoint - Careers Advice Blog. https://social.hays.com/2021/10/08/developing-mental-toughness/

Sutton, J. (2024, April). Boosting Mental Toughness in Young Athletes & 20 Strategies. PositivePsychology.com. https://positivepsychology.com/mental-toughness-for-young-athletes/

Taylor, A. (2021, September 9). A Tangible Example of Emotional Intelligence in Real Life - Directions Coaching. Directions Coaching. https://directions-coaching.com/2021/09/09/2765/

The Relationship Between Emotional Intelligence and Mental Health. (n.d.). Retrieved from BrainsWay: https://www.brainsway.com/knowledge-center/the-relationship-between-emotional-intelligence-and-mental-health/

Urquijo, I., Extremera, N., & Azanza, G. (2019). The Contribution of Emotional Intelligence to Career Success: Beyond Personality Traits. International Journal of Environmental Research and Public Health/International Journal of Environmental Research and Public Health, *16*(23), 4809–4809. https://doi.org/10.3390/ijerph16234809

U.S. Department of Veterans Affairs. (2021). Burnout and resilience: Frequently asked questions. Whole Health Library. https://www.va.gov/wholehealth-library/burnout-resilience.asp

Wallbridge, A. (2023, February 27). The Importance of Self-Awareness in

Emotional Intelligence. TSW Training. https://www.tsw.co.uk/blog/leadership-and-management/self-awareness-in-emotional-intelligence/

Walker, R. (2017). The Captain Class: A New Theory of Leadership. Random House.

Ying Lin, J. M. (2017, August 11). *Mental Toughness and Individual Differences in Learning, Educational and Work* Performance, *Psychological Well-being, and Personality: A Systematic Review*. Retrieved from NCBI: https://www.ncbi.nlm.nih.gov/pmc/articles/PMC5554528/

Learn more about Dr. Jeff D. Standridge

LinkedIn:	http://linkedin.com/in/jeffstandridge
Facebook:	@Jeff.Standridge
Instagram:	@Jeff_Standridge
Website:	www.JeffStandridge.com
Other:	www.InnovationJunkie.com
	www.ARConductor.org/Jeff-Standridge
	www.Amazon.com/author/JeffStandridge

www.ingramcontent.com/pod-product-compliance
Ingram Content Group UK Ltd.
Pitfield, Milton Keynes, MK11 3LW, UK
UKHW020419250726
13967UKWH00007B/2727

9 780977 934072